She, Her And Herself

OrangeBooks Publication

Smriti Nagar, Bhilai, Chhattisgarh - 490020

Website: **www.orangebooks.in**

© **Copyright, 2022, Author**

All rights reserved. No part of this book may be reproduced, stored in a retrieval system, or transmitted, in any form by any means, electronic, mechanical, magnetic, optical, chemical, manual, photocopying, recording or otherwise, without the prior written consent of its writer.

First Edition, 2022

She, Her & Herself

Sreeja Bayanagari

OrangeBooks Publication
www.orangebooks.in

This novel is solely to

all those who never had confidence in reading / finishing a complete book.

all those who feel / felt, one needs excellent diction to read a book
(which need not be the case)

all those who love LOVE and humor.

My work is dedicated to all the late bloomers out there. Life is a roller coaster ride. Hence, just accept it and stop expecting it.

A couple raised a kid- a female who was born with erudite abilities. She was always an eight years old at four years...a fifteen years at eight years... a twenty-five years old at thirteen years... Well, she was a pain in the arse for her parents. That's how they felt for a few minutes, hours, months, and years. She had to handle all of this, her studies, criticism, racism, and a lot more but found humor as escapism. Well, the plot is a decent blend of a student's life, love, amazeballs-moments and humor. It definitely leaves you teary-eyed.

Sweet Note 1: I had and have a thing with names since my childhood. Not that I hate them, but it's something like a weird bond that I maintain with *names*. Hence I snatched that habit and reflected it in my book. You will know it soon. Have a wonderful journey with my book!

Sweet Note 2: I hated reading with a dictionary beside. It used to distract my attention and focus. So, I gave you a few *Easy References* Section for your comfort. Read and chill with my plot!

Sweet Note 3: Nothing much. Meet you on the last page!

Easy References ....!!!

She – The girl... the kid... my protagonist!

She with an Uppercase S even in the middle of a phrase is the hint for my *fictional character*.

To each their own – According to their wish

Hitherto – till date

HAC – Her Amazement Club

Cliché – the routine

Harbinger – Signal/indication

SPL – School People Leader

JIC – Just in case

Eavesdrop – To spy; listen secretly

PMS – Premenstrual Syndrome

Rishta – Matches for a wedding (In Hindi)

Bizarre – Strange

Index

Easy References

Chapter- 1 1

Chapter- 2 80

Chapter- 3 137

Acknowledgements.. 171

Chapter- 1

She landed in 1996 may be on Monday, Tuesday or someday. Little did she know that the world was going to revolutionize in many aspects, not because of her birth though.

She was the most pampered grand kid according to her cousins. Again little did they know that her family (tree) had many expectations from her. So basically She got stuck in this hula hoop. Well her life was commingled with a bunch of emotions, confusion, and hilarious outcomes.

One fine morning... one day....... Naaah! Let us just get into the plot. Maybe she was the only kid/human alive who was more than overwhelmed on her first day at school. And that is how she amazed her parents for the first time which was one among many other times that she had. She ran to the restroom and got her refreshments done. Then she rushed to her mother for a quick brekkie and yelled at her father to drop her off as she had just ten minutes left to reach school (by the way, it hardly takes five minutes to reach). Her father was proud of Her like any other typical Indian father's

"Meri beti bahut acche se padti hai" feeling. Little did She knew what was coming in a few years. Don't hurry, readers! More chapters to come. (Well! The only way I could include suspense in my loopy plot). She enjoyed her first day so great that she did not want to go back to her place. Wait! Her age was like what... Five years? Oh yes! That was her pre-first grade. She was too much into her studies that she begged for more homework from her tutors. Again here come the teachers and tutors joining the Amazement Club of Hers. But what did that five-year-old kid think of life, education or career? Wasn't she too young and amateur for all of these? Maybe or maybe not. But definitely, she hated cartoons while her friends and kids of her age were stuck with the same. She loved video games like Road rash, Club, and Mario like a typical 90's kid. Thank God...! At least she had something in common! But her parents got irked and thought she should get admitted to a residential campus. In 2002 June, her life and worldview changed. By what? Should we need another chapter? Not really. Her life changed positively. She became more punctual, dedicated, and hardworking. Her diction and fluency in English proved that she was a pro. But was it a win-win for her parents? Not though... she was extra baggage when she came home for holidays. 8 Am - brekkie, 12 PM - lunch, 7 PM – Dinner; her mother felt like she was cooking for some army house. She could not handle that kind of punctuality and sincerity 24/7. She was confused if she should feel glad or sad when her daughter arrived home. As life is always like a weighing balance, her mother was happy that all her relatives and cousins just looked up to Her. But her mother could not wait for Sundays as those were the only moments she could spend with Her as part of the visiting hours policy at the campus. But back to Her Amazement Club (from now onwards, it's HAC), many new joiners have been observed. Every day she amazed one or the other at her campus. Her dad who never shed a tear, had to when he left her for the first time on campus. Her mother who never gave in to kids, had to do so for Her future and hence got convinced for the residential stay. But this little kid at the age of six never stopped trying though she hated her hostel. Too many restrictions, too many policies, and whatnot! She got jammed. She played the violin, learned brush painting, and played all kinds of sports she could. In fact, in her first grade itself, she almost had a fan club in her name. Half of the kids came to her for doubts and homework. Well, another amazing fact about her is that she even cleaned her dorms a lot that the aaya (cleaner) herself got shocked. She woke up way before the wardens and set her bed. The wardens got so bored of this kid that they called Her parents to know if she is immature or over-matured. Basically, she was not a normal kid from anyone's perspective there. Maybe at least we (readers) should treat her like a normal person. Well, this lady should pay me for that...! One fine day, she was listening to a class, and she could peep through the windows it was her grand pa. And recalling the shockers she gives, she did not fail this time either. In fact, she stood up and yelled at her grand pa not to disturb Her and asked him to wait till noon (which was not less than three hrs.). And as usual, her grand pa never came to the campus after that; not because he got irked but because he was scared or embarrassed somehow. Or maybe he, too, felt that he should be busy like that six-year-old kid. She loved the mess timings not just to eat food but to serve kids whilst none has ever taught her that. She picked up all the differences on her own. One should not be surprised if she flies or does magic. She waited for Sundays desperately to meet relatives, parents and outsiders. And other than all of those, she waited to meet her friends' parents too. In fact, her mother was jealous of the fact that She spent more time with others rather than with her. But, Her mother was satisfied with the fact that the entire campus and the officials loved her kid. One day there was an IQ test which was an eye-catcher for all those who participated and conducted too. This smarty could count the letters of around 10-11 sentences (on an average of 7 words/sentence) in less than 80 seconds while her competitors took more than 7 minutes. Not sure if this was an achievement, but definitely normal living beings couldn't count that fast. So, was this girl upgraded to 3rd or 4th grade?

Major reminder: This is a book with fiction for sure but not a feature film for such magical wonders.

She had to go through each grade as usual. Thanks to her parents who were never normal with such upgrades.

One fine day...

Her: Ma'am, can I suggest a way to solve this puzzle? (Written on the whiteboard)

Ma'am: Yes, but make sure you don't fail at it.

Her: Okay, then I won't.

Ma'am: I knew you were a coward.

Her: Maybe, and hence I am not able to solve it on the board while I could do it on my paper.

Ma'am was............... Arrrrrrrr .... Shocked again!

Maybe Her HAC should stop admitting people in.

And it would be boring to include similar instances that she had with a Violin tutor, Painting teacher, and Warden. So, it should be left to your creativity/imagination (Well, if you guys have time for it).

She used to have surprise visits from her father way too much as her father pampered her a lot back at home. He used the travel or distance factors at their best and always gave excuses to his business to meet Her regularly. Slowly, She became famous in the school as her father had a business deal with the campus for the supply of food and raw materials. She was in fact everywhere on the campus. As one could ever imagine, she was hyperactive, smart, and yes baggage for sure to the people around her (punctuality and dedication). But the fact was none could avoid her as she was a great learning source for the surrounding ones.

When the days just flew through her first grade, she so badly wanted to be at home. Her mother could not wait a single moment from the time, she received her summer schedule. But reiterating the point, Her mother was scared and so were the maids. They always get on High alert mode when She is home. A single mistake assured the person getting penalized as some Brigadier does to his lower officials. There is no Monday or Sunday or maybe there is no existence of any specific day or occasion when She is home.

For example, one fine day her cousins visited her place to play and chill with her. Her parents were proud of themselves that they could smartly hide Her weird behaviour from at least her relatives. But little did they know that they were not smart enough to do the same for years. Hence the D day arrived where spilling of beans happened naturally. Her mother was around with them 24/7 to handle any awkward situations. In fact, Her parents acted like bouncers to keep Her away from all the criticism that She might face. But again, she was clever enough to have the cards on her side. If she could get admired by an entire campus, that was the easiest for her in fact. Getting into the fun part...

Her: Let's play Club on my desktop.

Relative 1: No. I want to play hopscotch.

Her: Why do you have to play such stupid games in which you cannot grow your mind?

Her mother rushed to her rescue before anyone could throw comments.

Mother: Lil one! What She meant was that her desktop is a new one and she wants all of you to see and play on it.

Her: No. I didn't mean it that way. What I wanted to say was…..

Bouncer 2 was on his way… Well, Her father took the cue now. He rushed and asked the kids to come out and watch the rain. Little did Her parents know that they got promoted to the Bouncer Club from HAC. Her mother smirked at him and thanked him (inside) as that has been their new way of living since She was born or completed her five to six years or……!

She was enjoying her life so much that she ignored what Her parents had to go through (In Fact, they never had to if they hadn't had such embarrassment in them). Outings with family, friends, cousins or known ones made sure they had Her back.

Another fine morning she accompanied her dad to his office. He was caught up for the day, and hence he made sure that She should not irk him with Her stupid doubts that ultimately arose due to her Extra Intelligence! Once the deal was made, Her father could breathe. As soon as they reached the office, he had a meeting with some clients. Her father let her in too. She wore a blazer as She felt it would seem professional. But, Her father quickly took a glimpse at himself and then looked at her to remind her that he himself wore business casuals and also reminded her of the deal they had. Ultimately, she didn't utter a word and entered the office.

The day went too hectic for Her dad and once they returned, Her mother was waiting for them like never before. Not because she loved either of them that desperately but was bothered if anything went wrong in the meeting due to her *a-Lil-extra-smart* daughter.

Her entire schedule was a collation of smart thoughts, amazing days, a myriad of talents, dedicated decisions, and ideas. Her three years of schooling (1-3 grades) went similarly. Of course, many brilliant events were included in her three years journey. I don't want to bore you, people, by mentioning every such event. Her "Amazing others" might not be boring, but me mentioning it everywhere might be!

Slowly, as the years passed by, Her parents started shifting their expectations toward Her. They started buying more Video games than chocolates.

They started buying more books and fewer snacks. They started shopping for more clothes for themselves as their kid was weird towards that aspect of life. But to their surprise, she had a commonality with her mother (finally) that She was a great movie buff. In fact, there she nailed it better than her mom. She read a lot of magazines on movies and celebrities. She asked Her father to store all the cinema corners of the newspaper separately. But little did they know why she was so much interested in movies. This kid was more into the production department in order to cut down the budget. She was shocked and amused at the way movies were being made through huge investments. She did not leave much time for her parents to be happy as they were very thrilled looking at her diverting from Nerd Mode.

Their motto changed and became "Never be too thrilled as the kids are way beyond what we expect from them, every time." They didn't know whether to feel happy, awkward, sad or proud. They were always confused!

Finally, her mother made a big decision in her life (In fact in her daughter's life) to get her out of residential mode and make Her a day scholar. She was more than excited to change her campus. This kid always wanted new faces and new energies. And for sure, She had been bored with those surroundings for the past three years. That summer vacation was a great period for the entire family as She wanted to travel finally. Her parents felt like they were taken on some vacation by their parents and were more thrilled like kids. But, Her mother digested the fact that things were not smooth enough with Her around. And maybe, she jinxed her own happiness as the kid came running to her parents, mentioning a museum during the vacation (which was already boring for Her parents).

Her mom went like, "Arrrrrrr"

Her father screamed, "OMG"

The kid wanted to stay outdoors and enjoy nature, whereas Her parents wanted to book a luxurious hotel and enjoy the ambience. The trip had great memories for Her, but not sure if it was the same for Her parents. They felt like going back was way better! But what made them feel that way?

Well, a few instances including Her carrying a notebook to the museum and jotting down pointers like a nerd embarrassed Her parents a lot, and Her way of having meals with pets around (the better one when it came to embarrassing but again a boring one), Her early-rising habit was fine unless She woke others up. Her-missing-school feelings and conversations were shared with people around. And yes, those were definitely followed by other visitors, urging them to avoid the entire family. Leaving the rest to your imagination. But a hint can be provided "Her parents felt home and the army feels better than tripping with Her."

Expectations: A trip with a decent hotel and hospitality, rides, food and touring.

Reality: Embarrassment all over that ain't bad altogether but not good, for sure.

The entire summer vacation went not bad. As usual, Her parents had to survive it by managing and whatnot! It was June, and Yes… the happiest month for the kid! She could not stop torturing Her parents to take her to school as she loved purchasing new books every year. And in parallel with that, she enjoyed wrapping the books using book covers and labels and jotting down proverbs. That was a mental thing for other kids, for sure (Simply said, they hated it). Once the books arrived, as it was an orthodox family, Her father placed all the books for Pooja, and unfortunately (for the kid and fortunately for them), turmeric and other Pooja stuff got spilled over the books. This event was followed by screaming, drama, yelling, convincing, forgiving (forcefully), and all the emotions you can dump here! Finally, D-day arrived and she was all set to explore things at school. She entered the class and spoke to people around her. She made friends with as many as possible, impressed most of the staff and faculty, and explored clubs and library corners. Well, She did more than a fourth-grade kid does (not surprisingly). Just to remind you guys, HAC was still banging on! The more time she spent with others, the more members joined the club. But something unusual happened this time. Finally, she found her competitors, but unsurprisingly they were in other grades (to clarify, they were Her seniors). Let's add this unusual happening on the event list. Her father received a call from the school and was invited to speak to the Principal. Like regular fathers, he wasn't shocked as he knew She was always beyond what he or his wife expected Her to be. The next day he visited the campus and got a chance to speak to a lot of faculty that he never encountered, even when he was a kid or student. In fact, knowing that She was an ex-residential campus student and was from a great learning background, the Principal approached Her father and Her for suggestions on how to improve the activities at school.

Her father in his head: *What even? Whom did I give birth? Was I this talented? At Least 40%? No… Not at allllllllll. What has this kid done to the Principal?*

There was no response from hims, but yeah… the kid almost finished explaining things to the Principal before Her father even digested all of the stuff happening around. By the time he became conscious about it, he could not utter a single word as he knew he was good at handling clients, but not at these!

Note: Make a note that she was at a residential campus which was well-known worldwide. And to bring to your notice that only 10% of lakhs of applicants every year get admitted into it.

Maybe the note helps you decipher the fact of how good She was.

The new school welcomed her like some VIP or a celeb. She got extra attention from students, faculty, and every human around. They were shocked by the way she performed things. She was elected as a class representative anonymously in the very first week of her arrival. A club was formed after receiving her ideas and initiatives. Well unsurprisingly, her parents were hunting for the best doctors in the town to get Her checked, JIC. They were perplexed 24/7 as usual but simultaneously worried if they were missing out on something. It was like a typical scenario in Young Sheldon Part 3 (If you guys have time, definitely recommended from my end to watch). One fine afternoon, she was walking on the ground; her PT teacher called her and asked her about her favourite sport. Yes… this conversation was more than hilarious!

Her: Good Noon, Sir!

PT Teacher: Noon, Kid! What are you up to? Why are you roaming here?

Her: Nature lover.

PT Teacher: Well… do you play any specific sport? Any favourite one?

Her: Not really. I don't prefer playing much, but I love video games.

PT Teacher: What? You are a fourth-grade kid and you don't prefer it? You are not full-grown. Do you realize it?

Her: I do. But I am blessed to stay smarter than others of my age, and hence you, too, paid attention to me while I walked alone on the ground.

PT Teacher: This attitude won't keep you longer. You have to change a lot.

Her: No. I won't change and won't stop inspiring my friends. Don't feel bad, sir. I will surely play someday.

PT Teacher: I ain't feeling bad but worried about you.

Her: Thanks for that, but let me remind you of one thing if I start playing sports none will be able to play along with me due to my strict rules. They will give in to the sports they have been playing for many years.

PT Teacher and She went on a bet and played kho-kho; soon, the entire clan left and ran away. He then realized how precise the kid was and never dared to call her back. He liked Her but had to avoid her as she was too much to have around. (Welcome to HAC !)

She went back home and proudly cited the incident that happened in the school that day. She was so happy for the first time (God knows Her feelings and patterns). She did not feel that proud ever before. Her parents looked at her and listened to the entire conversation, having many things running through their heads. I wish I could present a few slides here. (Welcome to an MBA Grad life).

Example:- A doctor, a principal, a PT teacher, a full-grown kid, lots of her fans(students), staff, maids, et cetera were questioning Her mom and Pa. All of them were surrounded by mixed feelings (anger, excitement, irritation, and many more!) For the very first time, her mom regretted getting Her out of the hostel. She called her family friend who is a shrink and asked for an appointment, but this time it was not for her kid but for her husband. Yes... All that while, they hunted doctors for themselves too. But little did they know that they should have tackled the problem differently. Finally, they had a celebration ahead like a getaway from Her wonders. It was Her father's birthday in a few days. She wanted to surprise him for sure and went to Her mom to discuss the same. Her mother switched on the AC, opened the windows, and tried for the maximum ventilation possible to get into the room. (Her ideas were suffocating and intense for Her mom). But to her surprise, she loved Her plan and approved it. She felt happy that her kid was a normal one for at least a few moments.

The D-day arrived and all relatives too. And the Bouncer Club was back with a bang! This time Her mom accompanied her everywhere. The more famous her kid was, the more responsibility for her to take care of it. Then the day went well, including the party, snacks, (a high tea time party) relatives, and conversations. Her mother felt the day very normal and relaxing as her days generally included a lot of covering up shit, and making up stories to protect her kid. One year passed by as the last few Grades of Her's went by. She was promoted to the fifth Grade as if that needed any approvals/proofs for this at smart ass. Her fourth class faculty and staff were more than overwhelmed as they need not answer any more weird questions or maybe the toughest they had ever faced. Summer Vacation was there, but this time it was different as the kid finally decided to do some film making workshops; to be precise enough she went for a photography course. And this way, she offered her parents some relaxation and freedom as the workshops were residential. But again, She was not ready for any more hostel life post this. Hence Her parents enjoyed it to the fullest while she worked her best for filmmaking. Annual day occasion popped up between the vacation. All the parents received their kids' achievements and awards (if any) in the list appended to the invitation. It was going to happen in a few days, and Her parents decided to bring her back from the workshop as Her presence was mandatory (as claimed by the Principal).

The Annual Day arrived, and it commenced with amazing art presentations by kids. It had a good blend of dances, drama series, magic shows, and sports. All the kids were having a blast while She was waiting for the awards section. Once the same anchored, She ended up receiving, obviously, the most and the best. In fact, a new award was added this year, and it was termed "The All-rounder of the year". Maybe the school was stingy enough to give one award naming it differently rather than losing too many to the same student. She won it and was not overwhelmed, but yes, she did wait for this moment so that she caught the attention of everyone (who had not given her yet). Her parents were asked to give a winning speech, but Her mother denied it and forced Her father for the same. Forcefully, he reached the podium and took the mic with a quivering head and body. He wasn't sure what to say as he didn't get the award. He and his wife honestly had no clue about their kid to mention. In fact, these were the ones who wanted to see as shrink to decode the magic inside Her. But

Her father was cunning enough to manage it and said a few lines that took years for the parents to decipher. They left the campus and carefully stored the award. Not to make sure nothing happened to it, but to avoid attention from visitors as they will be shocked looking at a fourth Grade (Phew! Promoted to fifth...), achieving all of that. Vacation passed by... workshops passed by... award-winning speech was given... obviously by her father . Now, she was in fifth Grade. She started calculating the number of days left to reach her Degree. While Her mom asked her about the maths and the reason behind it, the kid mentioned the same, and her mom just had to make sure her BP or other health issues would not fluctuate. She ran to her husband and shared about it and then Her father came running to Her. After finding out the number of days, he could not imagine how that Lil master would be grown into when she reached that particular day!!! In Fact, he had an image of a bald head, oldie, old wife, bedridden, and yes more to it! She explained the reason behind it that she would get 100% freedom once she reached that level.

Her mom and dad in their heads: *As if anyone is stopping you now or as if anyone can!!!!!*

Her new class, same old kids, new faculty and new books; the patterns remained the same. But, she changed her mind set a lot. It seemed like she had a growth mind set rather than a fixed one. She started swimming, sports, dancing and many more. It was not because she was interested or passionate about it, but She wanted to lose weight and reduce the Vacation fat deposits. Her parents were clueless about it; all that mattered to them was to enjoy taking her to different classes. They never wanted Her to be a nerd, but little did they know she was way beyond that. She was that "Lateral thinking" or "out of the box" kid. Maybe that was the reason even Her parents could not decipher her skills. She read newspapers, socialized better, and ate a lot of junk food. In Her parents' perspective, she was becoming a normal kid day by day. But this was a phase she wanted to be in and not forced to be, unlike other kids. She became the school house leader (Red House; only 90's kids can relate to this). She grew tall and now, she seemed like an even more mature person to her parents. They were happy for the former one, but definitely not for the latter one. One fine day, she went to her dad and asked for a desktop as she wanted to learn excel and typing. Her father never said no to purchasing things that way. He, in fact, appointed tutors to take special classes. And, She started learning her mother tongue too. Yes, that was the area in which she was not a pro. It was not because she didn't try but she wasn't given that scope. Recalling to the point, She was in an International Residential School for the first three Grades. Though she had a year after that to learn, but never gave importance to the same. But now, She was watching Regional TV channels, News channels, and many more until She got a grip over Her language.

One fine day, She was announced as the Captain of the School badminton team. Her dedication to the game made the same PT teacher (who was pissed off with her attitude) announce her as the head of the game. She played for the State, but She had to give in to the game after a few months due to health barriers. Though She had the capacity to get back to the game and grew stronger, She never focused on the same. She explored other games. A weirdo, but a unique personality!

Fact... Too much diversion from her studies...!! I might have diverted but not her... Well, this Lil kid makes me think about many aspects of Her...Too hectic!!!

Traversing back to her study life, as usual, she was doing great. One fine day She visited a newspaper printing location of a brand, being a part of the school field trip. Post the tour, She brought her friends home. To her parents' surprise, that was the first time She did something like that. Though She was an extrovert, she never gave that importance to social life.

Wait...! What was the reason for this major shift? Nothing dramatic. Neither do I prefer mentioning the drama aspect of Her life. As mentioned earlier, that was a phase of her life and she chose that rather than being told or forced into it. She was enjoying it and little did she know that was something expected from her parents.

Slowly, years passed through Her achieving things, applause, and appreciation and it was not surprising to her anymore. She was in seventh Grade when she became the School Librarian and Team Captain of three or four sports (No intention to bore you guys at all by mentioning the names). But as every girl might have faced a Crush Staring phase in her life, so has She. There was a set of cute moments she waited for every day during her classes. Even the guy stared at Her for more than minutes and hours. She blushed a lot. (She wished

Her mom would be there at the moment, and definitely, Her mom wouldn't react any other way except being happy. Not because she would prefer this but because all she wanted was to see her kid as a normal one.) Sadly, this is how we get to prove we are normal! Phew!

Social Studies and English classes were the most interesting to her as they sat side by side, coincidentally. We can not expect co-ed to be that free in India! They helped each other with exams and assignments, and submitted projects together by teaming up with other classmates. They made sure they were always together in studies and other bondings though. He made sure none criticized Her (which she had been facing for ages). She had almost all of her cousins in the same school by the time she reached seventh Grade and hence proved the spreading of rumours of her craziness or weirdness! But She had her priorities this time, to stay over diligent about her career, to stare at him, to be Extra superb like a messiah maybe!!! Exams approached, and She helped him excel in most of them. For a moment, She realized how she changed, be it helping in exams, staring, smirking, blushing, Lil over-obsessed with her looks and dresses. Her mom enjoyed this phase more than anyone. She did not stop shopping for dresses, shoes, and sliders; she gathered all the new stuff that she could. He came on bikes and cycles near Her stay to have a look and there were harbingers (horn…honk honk!!) to alert Her. And here was when she used Her new dresses as there was no scope to wear civil wear at school. She used to run into Her room and change which amazed Her mom for sure; this time Her father too. That was the only amazement period they preferred or liked maybe. Hitherto, they were amazed but never liked it, in fact, that made them run for shrink hunting. But they were unaware of the reason behind that typical behavioural change in Her daughter. They would have hated it more if they were pensive about it. In fact, the entire clan enjoyed the phase. Carpe diem! Godspeed! But there were few instances where She avoided him as a typical female does..! Any guesses?

Instances go this way….!
Staring at other girls.
Giving importance to other humans.
Not appreciating enough.

Slowly, the kid was migrating to a perfect girl (maybe). There was this transitive relation going on in Her life. Knowingly or unknowingly…He changed her a lot….She changed ….this impressed Her parents. They even forgot about her educational aspects like rank, marks, and all. But She made sure she never gave in to that. Another year passed by and now, She got her monthlies and puberty. This attraction paved the way for infatuation and even more. Not being dramatic but that's how Women get more emotionally connected to their liking. There is nothing wrong with accepting this at all. They suffer only when they face egoistic men. (Feminism in me, at times, gets puked this way ...!) Slowly, She was called the all-rounder, the gang leader (yes, all of the other classmates ate and roamed alongside her), street smart, and all that, she deserved to be called. There was no more scope for her cousins to spread bizarre rumours.

Again, as tears follow smiles, that year changed Her a lot. The kid who grew up staying headstrong and stubborn about what she wanted was no more of that kind. Her family was shifting to a city from the current town they stayed. She knew very well what was going to happen. For the very first time, she got emotionally connected not only to Him but to many other kids. For a moment, She felt like she was going to lose all of the fame she built for years in the school and neighbourhood. It will take more years to build and even tougher to find such closed ones after moving to a new city. Her emotional synergy with them took her down for many weeks. Maybe that was her mini phase of facing lows as I do not prefer calling it depression. She fought with Her parents for days, hours, weeks, and more! Her parents were confused about Her behaviour as she was that kid who was resilient and adaptable to things. She usually never expected or demanded things from her surroundings, except this time.

Finally, the day to leave Her hometown arrived which was preceded by Her not mentioning it to any of Her closed ones, including the Staring Guy (Felt pathetic to call him this way though). It was just a shocker for all her closed ones. The only way they knew about Her was through Facebook where She was active enough. All of them connected to each other on the same platform. They created groups, texted and updated each other about their lives. But, She always waited for His friend request that never arrived. She did move on from the fact of waiting for Him and his messages, but it took Hera few months for the same. She joined a new school in her locality. It was her ninth Grade with all new faces, customs and lifestyles. Well, She did shift to a city from a town at an early age. It takes time, kids!!! But, Her HAC was always alive. Maybe the location or trends changed, but not her attitude and skill set. They only aged better with minutes, days, and years. She was from a town, to be precise, from an area where lifestyle wasn't given much importance which included dressing, eating habits, fluency, and many more. Though She nailed being fluent, at dressing, and definitely at being Street-smart, there were few aspects where She felt left out.

Her first day went like a roller coaster ride.

She entered the class and grabbed stares from others. In her head —- "Well, I know I look great. Stop staring. I bought this from a place where none of you can afford to buy it. I know I have a great walking style and attitude. Stop it, Guys" The reality check went this way — Tears welled up at the end of the day. She hated the class, people, school, and every inch of the new place. Her parents, for the very first time, had no clue about Her tears (Well, they had never witnessed that aspect of her). But, She opened up to her mom.

Mom: What happened champ?

Her: Mom...

Mom: Why are you upset? Why do you seem low?

Her: Actually...

Mom: New vibes didn't feel like a cynosure, I suppose. Is that right?

No reply for two minutes. Her mom started again with the same dramatic questioning.

Her: Stop it. Can you pause? You ain't giving me space to speak up for the past few moments. You are continuously questioning me, mom!! Pause... Pause... Stop! Let me puke out shit.

Yes, I am upset. Yes, I do not like the vibes here. Yes, I am the lowest person now. Not because your daughter is afraid of humans here but of facing fascism and racism way, too much. I feel like I have left all my jewels back in town. My true vibes... My true clan and people... I miss all of them!!!

Pin drop silence. Jaw-dropping shocks. Mom and Pa were in surprise and sadness.

Her Pa approached her and asked Her what exactly made Her feel that way. She went on like a running bus... did not stop, and never went to stop at all.

"I have no clue. As soon as I entered the class, I grabbed a lot of attention. Little did I know that those were weird stares and glares. No one even came up to me or cared enough to sit beside me. I thought I should start conversing and take the initiative. Then, none replied. They were so dumb to even respond; in fact, mules!! I got irked and sat silent. Then a girl came to my rescue and asked about my oily hair. I was shocked receiving such loopy questions. I didn't care to respond. Then another guy came. I asked him if it was the oily hair, but he had no clue about it and mentioned that he stared at me for my fluency, in a good way though. I decided to sit with him throughout the day as I could get a few insights about the other idiotic kids there. He mentioned the city culture to me about racism, fascism, domination, partying, judging others so easily, and many more. And then I got it that few stared at my oily hair, few at my complexion for sure, and others... God knows how to decipher them also!! But luckily, I found a few decent ones. There are darker kids than me too. What would they have gone through in their initial days in the city? That hit me hard, Pa."

He just gave a soft smile and hugged Her. He left without uttering a single word or phrase.

There were no dramatic dialogues or no sensitive angles.

Phew!!!!!!!

Her: Pa, what...?

Before she could even finish Her questioning, she could see him replying, "You are way beyond all of that, my champ!"

Now, that hit her even harder; maybe, hardest hit hitherto. She gained all the energy to get back at all of them at school. You can visualize Her as some Avenger (Marvel fans can relate a lot too, here) as that's how she imagined Herself. She got down from her bed, removed the spear from Her chest and felt like a self-bouncer, and walked away. Her mom laughed a lot inside but did not dare enough to smile it out. She felt the scenario stupid as she knew Her daughter was just missing the town way too much, and it was like a small triggering event for Her to puke out the pain.

Well... I wish all parents would have confidence in their kids this way. *Freedom*!

The next day started with an essay writing contest and an IQ test. She, as usual, nailed them; She got third in the entire city. *Worth it!* That is what she felt in Her head. She gave that kiddish stare to all of them and felt satiated deep down inside. That smirk, walking style, attitude, propensity to talk, and all of Her got moulded in seconds. Just a night changed Her, or just a hug and a smile changed Her!! She did some crazy acts like intentionally approaching other kids, asking for their scores, and hence followed by boasting about Her scores. She wasn't gaining their attention at all. TBH she was planning for something big as Her Pa mentioned that She was way beyond all of them. But Yes, everyone knew Her, shut their mouths, bowed to Her talents indirectly. She even became the School People Leader in a few weeks anonymously. That was the best way of proving... Getting back or self-answering ? I would not wonder if She chose all of them simultaneously.

For sure, HAC was alive through new entries not just from school but from neighborhood, family friends, strangers, new friends, and this time, cousins too. There was no more hiding and covering up stuff. She was grownup now (according to Her mom and Pa), and hence they had no issues letting their relatives know about her street-smart or so-called weird skills. Arghhhhh...! They still had not totally changed a few things would never , in fact! A new phase of life, a new way of voicing out opinions, a new aura, a new mind set of Her parents... every aspect of Her life seemed like celebrating New Year's eve! Phew!!!

She wanted to have a major focus in Her life when it came to her career and personal life. She started exploring guys, and indeed, She had to move on from the guy in town. She waited enough for His messages and calls. She deeply felt that a few things have to be two-way and not one-way which could be dangerous. So, She migrated her schedule towards social media every day for a few minutes. She sent friend requests to all the guys in Her class after the revenge was taken to get back at them. In fact, she did not mind being soft this way. Maybe she knew how to get balls on Her court. But, that went useless as none thought about Her or interacted with Her; I as if She would compromise here…For sure, never!! She knew how to get things done. At times, She was the most cunning one in the room if she chose to be. Days went similarly. She realized that she was admitted into a reputed institution, and Her tenth Grade exams were a few months away. Not surprisingly, in Her state preparation of tenth starts in ninth Grade itself, and don't even think, "What would happen about ninth studies?" Trust me! Leave it for the greater good. Believe me, guys! It just works this way. She thought why not use studies to divert her mind from the town guy rather than depending on another connection? She started targeting her board exams. She knew that she needed the hardest efforts to score well. It's similar to a Civils exam preparation for a kid of Her age. She gave her phase exams the best way she could and topped all the citywide practice exams, which were like a demo version of real exams. She gained all the confidence she could through these ranks and fame. She wasn't satiated though. Maybe she was a typical girl deep inside to forget the staring guy. But, this time, she decided to face it rather than hunting for distractions. She accepted the fact of missing him way too much, and more than Him missing her. She just patted herself (mentally) and memorized Her Pa's words. She pulled off the stunt again of walking with her head raised, and like a typical superhero… Apologies… Superwoman!

It was mid-November; the preparations were going on for Annual Day. She had to be more accountable to each event, participant and sponsors. After becoming the School People Leader, that was the first time for Her to Head an event. She had no chance of giving in to that responsibility due to Her hectic study schedule. She had back to back meetings with faculty, event organizers, and other student councils. It was a hula hoop for Her. But, She enjoyed it a lot. When She craved for diversions, there were none, but now, it came uninvited; She enjoyed that fact even more than the event. There was a list of events on the cue, like dance, drama, film workshops, photo booths, and food stalls. In fact, She used all her past (International) school standards to improve the current scenario. She worked on designing concepts, science projects, and trade fairs. She wanted all of them to be part of the Annual day function. Her sponsors were more than thrilled, looking at a fifteen-year-old kid executing them. It was indeed a cynosure for all the humans around Her to watch her and listen to Her. The day arrived, and She received her ID card for the very first time. She was overwhelmed looking at it. Carrying an ID card wasn't the first time, but such a huge responsibility to Head a school's major event was definitely the first time. That happened no less than a few months after she arrived in the city.

What would Her mom do, and what about Her Pa?

Well, her mom was busy with all-mom-gatherings (kitty party), and she boasted a lot about Her kid as usual. She even stole the ID card for a while to flaunt in front of her new friends. She gained a lot of attention indeed. Her Pa got busy with his business…new location… new clientele… better targets… turnover… all Biz terms could be dumped here though. But, as if he compromised in boasting about his kid's achievements. There was a constant heavy competition between both of them in flaunting Her skills and achievements. Bizarre! The same humans who were part of the Bouncer club (hiding her talents) were now, doing media work and promoting Her skills. The annual day went really well, and all the students did a splendid job executing it. The entire landmark of the school heard and watched the event. It became famous in the street with innovations and ideas. Gramercy, Lil champ! Maybe Lil should be erased from now on. Well, She was a grownup girl now.

That night was the most memorable to Her indeed. But, again, not because of anything related to the Annual day (Of course, She felt glad about it), but chats. Chats??? What were those? Yes... She felt like relaxing a bit from Her hectic schedule and juggling between classes, preparation, phase exams, event organizing, and what not!! And, She ended up in front of her desktop to chat with her friends. It had been months since She was active on the same. So, she was thrilled to see all the toaster notifications and seen zoned chats. To her amazement, She finally could see the town guy's request!!!. She got nervous and went blank; clueless about how to react. She had no idea if she was even conscious enough to react. Even if She was, how to react? If She even reacted, would he mind texting at all...? Non-stop question banker mode was on. She took a pause, ran to the fridge and had water followed by a fulsome meal. Maybe, She wanted to calm herself through those but nothing worked. Hence She decided to accept the request, but a girl's ego never dies though… She texted him by clicking the chat button. What was that message?

Hey.
How are you?
Long time.
Hello.
Who is this?

It belonged or related to none of these types. In fact, Her first ping went like "Are you the same guy who stared at me a lot in English classes or roamed around my house?" That's how she drained Her ego; She wanted to make sure there was no hacker doing this, or maybe, she wanted to make him realize the precious moments spent together. She did not receive a text back nor did she knew if he read the message. All She knew was that he would not know how She missed him way too much (if at all he had such queries running in his head all these days). Girls are egoistic that way, but worth it for all their PMS levels or the emotions, which they carry every day. Well, I am feministic that way. A few days passed by with no response. But, checking the chats was the first thing in Her day journal. She, with no fear or second thought, eagerly waited for his replies. Summer vacation arrived, and She was well aware that there were no more proper vacation holidays until She passed her twelfth Grade. It meant that She had to work hundred per cent for three more years. How pathetic the educational system was in her days. Couldn't agree more TBH! Studying three years to get into a good Bachelor's College... Not fair... Phew!!! Arghhhh......!

It was mid-May, and She had continuous coaching classes and phase exams. She hardly thought about the guy. Maybe, very few times, she thought all about them meeting secretly in the past days. Nothing beyond that, as She restricted herself not to give it a thought anymore, but again not to run away from Him. She became stronger year by year, minute by minute and grade by grade. The best part was that She realized the same. She even ended up writing a journal about him if She had no other option except to think about him, which was rare though. Her ranks were good; never compromising. Her sports went on well. According to Her, She had to play sports to stay fit. She never wanted a profession out of it. She even wanted to build abs which she thought about after watching TV shows, especially Friends; a show one could never miss. The show changed many lives of her known friend circles. She used to blush a lot watching Rachel and Ross (She and Him) and visualize a lot, in fact. This happened on a monthly basis during her PMS. She used to have crazy cravings to eat or to go hug him hard. She definitely wanted him back, though she would never accept that it's not two-way according to Her. She didn't want to end up like a desperate loner. Summer went by, in a similar manner.

It was her tenth Grade first day. She was like a kid going to her school for the first-time, blushing and overwhelmed. She was the topper of Her school in all phase exams. Her degree coaching classes were going as usual. She was the smartest kid on campus and the entire branch, in fact. Many students' parents approached Her parents to know more about the kid and her habits. Though all that had been happening for ages, it was different for Her this time. And, when her Mom asked her about the same she went like, "Mom! Do you realize that this is my last school year? Like, there is no more mention of 'My kid went to school', but it's gonna be like 'she went to college'. The college word itself thrills me a lot. It gives me a lot of chills." Her mom felt the moment cute, gave a smile, and left from there. Though her first day went monotonous, She ended her day well by chatting. Yes, finally, she received a text from Him though it wasn't of the level She expected it to be. But, who cares when he replied, at least. She forgot the world when She chatted with him. She got to know that he was studying on a residential campus in the same city. They exchanged their contact numbers and were on a call. They heard their voices after, like thousands of hours and hundreds of days. They shared a lot of information about each other which they might have missed out. He mentioned his new crush and dating life. Oops…! She thought she should stop right there at that moment. She got goosebumps and started sweating. But in a few minutes, She realized her worth and gave a positive response. Her Pa was in her head mentioning, "You are way beyond all of this." They ended up being good friends. And, soon enough She realized nothing was permanent around Her or Us. She understood that She wanted him around in her life and felt glad even if it was in the form of a friendship. She hated ghosting for sure. But, after a few weeks, She realized she no longer thought about him much now, as they talked to each other every day. So, basically, it was just an attraction-based love and not what She thought it to be. The emptiness She had been carrying all those days, got erased in a flash. Godspeed..!

She got busy with new friends and trends. She changed her hairdo, dressing a bit as soon as she realized that She could pull it off better that way. She hung out with many friends during Her free time. She started new habits, but never found an excuse to give in to previous ones. All of these went seamlessly parallel to Her hectic class schedule and coaching. She even started attending dancing classes, and the abacus (late, but not that late!!!). Every week of Her journal had all the talents which one wanted to explore. It wasn't easy and it even reached a level where Her parents themselves asked her to rest a bit. She was always found working like a robot, and one couldn't agree more. Her day started with morning brisk alongside Her Pa, classes, and two activities from the habit list for a day. Weekends went more hectic than a weekday, as She had lots of time to attend different classes. God! Life of a robot would have been better for sure. She never wanted to compromise any of the above for any factors that could exist in the world. Indeed, She was headstrong about it. She replaced laziness and excuses with all those activities that a human could do! She attended filmmaking workshops once a month which changed Her life a lot. (Later chapter guys!! Patience..! Phew!). To make it simple, She was leading a life no teenager or high teen would want to. Everyone would want not to study, not to be busy, not going for coaching classes daily. They wanted to sleep, laze around, watch movies; the exact opposite of what this kid wanted to do. Well, She was unique rather than weird or bizarre... I think we should address Her that way, at least after Her parents themselves stopped hiding her skills.

Days and months passed, by preceded a few events where She handed over the SPL responsibilities to a junior (that's how it works). She felt a bit emotional and gave precise training to her junior to make sure that the expectations of the Annual Day wouldn't go down or fade away. Her boards were close to a few fortnights. She was a bit tensed which was a human tendency again, and was very normal. Abnormal students have been preparing for the exams not for a year but two. It is like twice the effort you put in a year. Hence, come the expectations, it was Hers too. She seemed casual from out, not in, for sure. She had a gap of ten days to drill her learning before giving the final attempt which was generally mentioned, as a Preparation

Break. She focused majorly on Her weak subjects... Here, 'weak' meant scoring 80 on a 100. That's how she treated herself as weak where the same level was seen as a top score for others; too tough to beat Her in that! The break went well with her habits of not being ignored, as she was aware they would be ignored during Her examination days. Smart move, in fact. The final day was there. She had six subjects to finish in a span of fourteen days.

Exam day 1
Exam day 2
Exam day 3.

Final exam day!
I hope the actual exams would finish that way. Phew!

She was done with all her exams in a jiffy (that's how she felt). But, results took time, and She never gave much importance to them as She was confident about her efforts. Summer vacation was there; She could rest, but She wanted to learn horse riding this time. Tadaaaa… Her parents knew it was expensive, and they might not be able to afford that much. But, Her father never said no to her. Maybe, She took it a bit for granted, but very few times though. She woke up daily at 4 AM for the same, as the trainer was in high demand. He was busy like no one as it was summertime. Most of his students took the training during those two months. She was given just forty minutes slot in the early morning, and not much importance as none of Her age were there. She didn't mind all of these, as Her focus was on finishing the course. In fact, She reported fifteen minutes early to her slot; in case, she could get extra training. Ill-luck!!! The rest of the day, She spent on calls and chatting or other habits according to Her journal. She had prepared a journal for Her Pa to make his biz organized. He never followed it, though; even if he had to spend a maximum of three-four days. It was not because he was lazy, but to follow it was that tough. Imagine how organized Her journal might have been!! She even started cooking alongside Her mom as the latter kept ranting, "You never have time to spend with your mom. Peh!". Somewhere, She felt it was her responsibility to be fair to her parents. The grown-up mode!! A few weeks passed by, and She again received a text from the town guy. It was a random *Hello*. She see zoned his text though not because She was J or whatsoever typical reasons one can think of but She was caught with stuff. At least, that's how she convinced herself. She ended up replying after a day as Her head irked her a lot to reply. She replied saying *Sup*. The conversation went well, and he asked Her the reason for her late replies, which She ignored. She replied those messages, which made her feel strong and confident. Or maybe, she replied only those which she felt like replying, as simple as that. Soon, she realized the summertime came to its ending, which meant no more horse riding, at least for a while. And, it was that time for which she had been excited for months now. It had arrived finally, now!!!

She imagined herself being called a college girl, a totally grown-up girl, and more!!!! Just to remind the readers of her age, now She is sixteen years, pretty young and old enough. She bought a new college sling bag in which you could carry only three books maximum, which was way better than carrying 10 kg heavy ones since Grade 1. A typical educational system… Argghhh! She changed her room interior and got a more comfy chair alongside a table. She almost felt herself a new CEO or a professional promoted to a higher level hierarchy in an MNC. That's how she imagined herself every time. It was not overconfident but self-confident about herself and her skillset. She was stubborn that way though. While none of the teens, millennials, Gen Z, and zoomers had such unique confidence levels!! The rare breed…! Just to mention, She still was a day scholar, and she never wanted to go back to a residential phase because of Her extreme OCD levels. Those levels grew age by age, hour by hour and minute by minute. She ended up feeling it as a disease in fact, and Her parents too felt that way. The night before Her first day at college went bad, as she could not focus and stress-ate a lot of junk. She couldn't sleep either. She was on social media for the entire night. Those were all symptoms of an over-anxious person or an over-excited one. It's not that She wasn't aware of those symptoms, but She didn't give them much importance. She had her PMS too going on but she didn't want her first day to get affected due to the same. Girls' issues and problems are never-ending, and need a conscious response. Else they apologies... We end up facing impediments in every small adverse situation around us.

It was 4 AM which was like 11 PM, 12 AM, or maybe 4 PM to her. As she couldn't sleep last night, looking at the clock did not make a huge difference for Her; it just reminded Her to start the day. Nothing beyond that! She was restless but in constant mode to enjoy Her day, though. She got her refreshments done in a jiffy and got ready...

this time, in a colorful crop top paired with Her best jeans. Finally, a day arrived to get rid of Her school uniform. She enjoyed every moment, thinking about these major or minor shifts. All she wanted was a change from a monotonous and boring life. She didn't regret her past though. She was adaptable in Her best way. She had her brekkie, got into the car, and obviously, Her Pa was driving the car. She was grown up but not enough to drive her car. That's how Her Pa felt about her, at least. So did the Maa (mom). As soon as, She reached the campus, She jumped out of the car like a typical Tollywood or a Bollywood hero. Her Pa was shocked and ended up screaming at Her. As if she gave a damn. She smirked, waved at him, and asked him to leave. According to Her, none could understand her excitement levels. That had been Her belief for ages though. Hence, she stopped conveying her feelings, emotions, and anxiety to other humans, including Her mom and Pa. She saw all the girls and boys around Her and tried to capture if anyone stared at Her. No one did. Poor girl…! Peh..! But, that's not how she felt… She just told herself that all of these faces would end up staring at and admiring Her very soon. The class started, and She jotted down all the pointers and book references that needed to be focused on. She listened to every session as if She was going to crack IITs or NITs. Maybe she will, someday. Lunch break ended up weird, as She didn't get a company. It was almost similar to what she had faced during her first class when she moved to the city. But again this time, She was satiated that way. She thought of being an extrovert but again felt *it ain't worth it*. One had to be smart to be that way, not blind enough to follow it. She followed the same, which was succeeded by many people coming and introducing themselves to Her. She was a known figure by then as it's the same area where she did her ninth and tenth. Kids had seen her hoardings and ranks, Her leadership roles during annual day events. She had done all that she could do in Her life, and life had given a huge ROI to her this way (by then). They exchanged their contacts, social media handles, and other gossip too. It was a proper co-ed gang. They all became close enough in no less than a few hours. They planned to bunk the classes the next day (which was just the second day). Little did they know about Her, She gave a huge NO to that. No one even tried to convince Her as they got clarity by then on how stubborn and particular She was about a few things. The day ended well by exchanging notes, having high tea time snacks in a nearby bakery, and meeting faculty (It was just Her). She reached home, threw Her sling aside, and fell on the bed. She got a call from the intercom asking Her to come for dinner. They grew well in the past two months and had a few renovations done inside their home. Thanks to her Pa, who worked his tails off for that. Now, horse riding had become easy not because of the practice but because they could afford it easily. But, poor Her… She didn't have time though. Well…Life enjoys playing with our emotions that way. It was 7 PM, and She felt how hectic these IIT and NIT coachings are. She juxtaposed it with how she used to reach home at 5 PM during her school days. She felt bad that her habits would soon get affected due to this. But, She had no other option. It was the case with other students too, who are aspirants of IITs and NITs, indeed. They had to give in to their personal hygiene and habits for a while. That was the only aspect where She wanted to go back to her school days. Meh!

Her typical day started at 8 AM and went on up to 10 or 11 PM. She planned her days accordingly. She targeted top-notch institutions. Whilst, She always wanted to get a degree in a BBA campus rather than at a B-tech campus. She still chose the latter for Her Pa, who brainwashed and brainstormed

Her accordingly. She even had an option to swap careers after B-Tech. It's not like one has to stick to engineering jobs, post their BTech. Many had been biz magnates, post b-tech too. Hence, She targeted the same. She didn't mind giving up on Her personal hygiene or Me time for a while. In fact, most of Her priorities changed once She became a college girl. It was priority one... Study... Priority two... Study... Priority N... study...!

That's how she drilled her mind too. There were days when she woke up at 4 AM to grab extra hours to spend a bit of time for room cleaning or reading books. It was tough to compromise on these two factors. Once in a fortnight, She gave a few hours for these two. Her coaching had lots of phase exams almost fourfolds of her tenth exams in terms of attempts and toughness. But, all of those were accepted well by Her, as it was a challenging phase. She managed both the entrance exams schedule and state board exams. She did a day journal accordingly.

Her mom hated all of this though; as I can give you a few instances about typical Indian moms...!!

One fine day, She was studying at 6 AM, which was observed by Her mom. The day before that, the housemaid complained about Her hair falling to

Her mom. Maid ended up showing the tangled bunch of hair to the latter. Her mom was about to faint. She had no clue. She wanted good rishtas (marriage hunting) for her kid, which meant that She should be good-looking and would have thick hair. Her mom had already compromised on the complexion factor as Her kid is dark-skinned (but thick-skinned for sure). She was scared even discussing the racism, but couldn't help as that's how rishtas approached girls. Most Indian groom-families need good and fair-skinned girls. That's the fact! All of these played in her head in a jiffy; she ran to her kid and asked Her to rest. The conversation went this way……

Mom: Kid… sleep!

Her: Mom… I'm not a kid anymore. Stop calling me that! And, no I can't sleep. I woke up not to doze off.

Mom: I know about your hair fall issues. The maid has shown me all the bunches. This is my major concern and not your exams at all. If you really feel like you are grown up, then you should be able to understand what I am trying to convey.

Her: I know I am smart, but not smart enough to understand your indirect convos. Be clear and leave my room before I call Pa.

Mom: You have become so stubborn and stupid too. How will I get rishtas for you if you go bald at sixteen years?

Arghhhhh…!! Pa from the other room came running after eavesdropping on the conversation. He felt he should have come a bit early. He shouted at Her mom and asked her to leave. He and his kid felt deaf for a moment. Typical moms focus on their kid's marriages more than careers for sure. Her mom felt it took at least four-five years to get a good groom. She wanted her kid to get married at 23, as it's an ideal age for any girl to get married. And, hence her preparation stage one had started now which meant taking care of her kid's beauty. Hence proved!!! If you guys are shocked, that's how it works in most Indian typical households. I ain't an exception to this as I faced this similarly. Pretty sure about most of the girls or moms, reading this, might have been part of this play. It took a few days for Her to move on from the above conversation, and She even stopped talking to her mom for a while. She stopped eating at home. She had her brekkie from outside while Her dad dropped her in the college; lunch from the canteen and snacks from a bakery nearby college. Dinner was the only time, when she had to pull it off even better as She would be home, and there was no

Swiggy, back then. She had no clue but never wanted to compromise as Her mom should be taught a lesson. She ended up eating fruits as her supper for a few days. She constantly waited for mornings so that she could balance that hunger. Her dad knew these patterns and asked Her mom to apologize. But, her mom was not ready as she felt nothing wrong with the conversation. A few weeks passed by that way, and She found many friends who got lots of food for lunch. She had made many friends so that she could taste all of their lunch. It sounds weird and lame, but Hunger drives you crazy. In Her case, it's a combination of hunger and stubborn nature.

One fine day, post-college, at around 8 PM, She saw a plate of dinner with all her favorite dishes placed in her room. She had no clue, who placed it there. Obviously, it should be Her mom or Pa… as if that was a thriller genre. She ran to the door, locked it tight, and came back, running. And, she ate like never before. She satiated all the cravings she had for the past few weeks. She felt so good and realized to thank Her mom, as she was sure it was her mom who placed it there. But, the stubborn one took a stick note, inked it with Thanks, and placed it on the plate. Phew!!!! Few kids, too, never change; it is not about moms all the time. Well, it makes sense why stubborn kids have stubborn moms... Sorry, stubborn moms always have stubborn kids... Genes!! A few more weeks passed, and things got well, not because any of them apologized to each other, like they just got sorted by themselves, somehow. It just happens naturally. Weird, but it happens. Her mom never stopped giving attention to Her beauty nor has she stopped waking up at 5 AM, studying, and all her hectic schedules. Amazingly, even her hair follicles did not give in to falling off. Her hair fall went in a similarly, come what may. Box of three stubborn activities going simultaneously... the only human stuck her was Her Pa. Trying to pitch in whenever needed to maintain the peace. He did feel like a PM at times to peace out between nations. But, obvious PM for the house and not for even single square feet beyond that. She gave her practice exams well, and everything was going fine. She didn't miss Her workout sessions much as Her books were heavy. Though college life started with a few books, those were more than enough to weigh around 7-8 KGS! In that way, She felt, at least one of her habits did not need to be given into. Finally, Her eleventh finals approached, and she gave them by ending up with her face everywhere on hoardings. Usual... routine...

monotonous… casual… regular… You can name it which ever way you would want to.

She topped the city in eleventh boards. Not a small thing though! But, none of this excited her, not because it was regular, but She targeted the entrance exams, which were a year away. She even gave up on her summer vacation. Well, Her mom was back on the scene this time. She prepared a good schedule on her own for her kid, which included a *badam* pack for face, lemon pack for hair, brisk for 40 minutes, and it went on….! It sounded lame, but that's what happened. Why did not she include something like, de-tan packs…? Why fairness packs? Why did she show such Indirect Racism? Why couldn't she accept the current levels of melanin? ROFL… those could never be answered, not only by Her mom, but by other moms or other racists too. Demand me to write another book to elaborate on the same. Little did Her mom know that her schedule would not be on track. She might have forgotten about Her stubborn kid. Her mom ended up pasting the plan in Her room without her conscience. The day, She checked the plan, She wanted to tear it so badly and shout at Her mom, but this time, She wanted that to be different…. She never wanted to waste energy on changing her mom (which was never gonna happen). She just nodded to her mom this time which obviously left Her parents in shock. Though her mom wasn't sharp enough to grasp it, Her Pa knew his kid. He was sure there might be a backup plan in her kid's head. True that! She used to find a bowl of paste every morning and night in her bathroom as per the schedule. She threw all of that in the basin and came out after twenty minutes enacting the glow on her skin. Poor mom...! She didn't doubt her kid. She was happy about her plan working as planned. Her mom saw Her face every day and enjoyed the glow (IRL there is no pack or paste plan followed. It was the natural glow). She was so happy that her tan and hair fall was gone. Her hair fall had reduced (according to Her mom). But none of the schedules were followed. It was all about the mother's head and her thinking. She always saw her kid as dark-skinned and hence overlooked the natural glow. But, Her Pa knew the plan. She had one parent on her side for sure. Sometimes, it was Her mom and at times, Her Pa. The only part which was followed according to the plan was– brisk, as she honestly wanted to maintain her health. She couldn't agree more on that. Summer came to an end in a similar humorous manner.

The twelfth Grade became more hectic; more books, more timings, more efforts, and hence more hair fall…! The latter part was what Her mom calculated. But this time, Her patience levels were drained and almost faded. It was a legit stressful situation or maybe a phase in Her life hitherto. Her Pa was more concerned about her health this time. He didn't want to push her much into this. He had a conversation with her regarding the same.

Her: It's fine, Pa. I know that I always wanted a BBA. But trust me, I want to do this on my own, and later will do MBA.

Pa: I want to apologize for brainwashing you this way. You can still choose whatever you want. There are no more barriers that way. My assurance!

She gave a smile and left from there. She was so happy after that conversation. It was deep as she could grasp Her Pa's confidence in her. It was no more about the career choice but Her Pa's feeling that she could achieve it anywhere. She recalled her parents' faces in her head and could not stop laughing. It was a drastic difference between them like how Her mom wanted her fairness levels to be on point and Her Pa wanted her career to be on point. But she admired both of them equally as any other kid would do. Her mom as usual was searching for new techniques; this time, to get her height on point. Well, She was not short for sure, but Her mom was never satiated. Maybe, she would even ask Aishwarya Rai to apply some pack to improve her glow. The typical moms!!! Never stop looking at the black dots on white paper. Maybe, every girl will end up becoming a typical mom not this way, but in different ways. Godspeed!!!!

One regular day, she reached her campus. She was asked to leave immediately due to some riots going on around. She felt happy for the first time. She wanted to enjoy that *bunking college* mode. She never encouraged it or faced it. But, that was the result of her hectic schedule. It was too monotonous that she demanding that to herself. Finally!!!! A much-needed one though. That's how she felt. And, I am expecting all of you might be feeling the same… Phew!! She hung out at the bakery for about two hours. She had a posh tablet (electronic device) by then. Thanks to her rich Pa though. So, she opened a myriad of YouTube channels, connected her Bluetooth device to the tab and was in her zone. She was too occupied to pay attention to her phone, which was ringing with weird caller tunes that grabbed the attention of all visitors. Everyone gave her weird expressions. Few of them left once she got the second or third call. The manager of the bakery rushed to Her before he could lose other customers. He was very well aware that she had been a reliable and credible customer, but not at the risk of losing others. He somehow risked approaching. Generally, people get scared to disturb her when she was involved too much; be it Her mom, Pa, et cetera. It's not because she looked scary but Her aura worked that way. Well, that's how it looks, but God knows about humans these days. Even guys get mood swings like PMS... So, one never knows. She was not to stereotype that aspect but that's the fact! She felt like leaving as she got bored after a while, and she wanted to watch a movie, but none of Her friends was around. As She never gave time to them, so, felt it unfair to expect time from them. Suddenly, she realized that she had to check Her phone and the missed calls. She saw an unknown number, which gave her a ring many times. She had no clue about it, not that she cared enough. She ain't a call person anymore. She gave in to all other things due to lack of time. Twenty-four hours of Her was just about targeting reputed degree colleges. That break was taken after many months. She ended up going for the movie alone as she loved movies and books. She was tired of the latter and hence chose the former. She thoroughly enjoyed the movie, crew, snacks, and the entire aura. She returned home where She had to face a lot more. Her day just started. That's how she felt.

Her mom had been waiting for her desperately since evening but could not track Her kid's phone or movements. She saw Her and asked about the review (movie). She was in shock. She had no clue how her mom got to know.

Her: What??!!! Are you spying on me? Should I call Pa?

Mom: I am not scared of you or your Pa. Call him. Let him know about your bunking of college and other stuff you did.

Her: Why would you spy on me? Yes, I went to the movie. I didn't attend a single class. But the college was closed. Do you even know that? Do you care to ask me?

Mom: So what? Don't you have the minimum common sense to call me and inform me of the same? And with whom have you gone to the movie?

Her: Ask your spy !!

She left from there and banged the door so hard that their neighbours could hear. She just hated all of that. So, she took the plan stuck on the wall by her mom, tore it into pieces and threw it outside the door just to gain the attention of Her mom. Smart and egoistic kid!!! Her mom just could not handle all of this and called her Pa to come home ASAP. Her Pa was dead...! He was planning to come in a while but never wanted to, now; as if he had other options. Once he reached home. All of them were assembled in the drawing room. She sat in her bean bag, Her Pa was standing and Her mom was somewhere in the same room though. Stares and glares were exchanged among the three of them. It was like a serious thriller scenario. Her Pa begged about the issue. He wanted someone to speak up. SPY part 2 discussion continued...

Her: Your wife spied on me, today.

Mom: Your daughter bunked the college. And, there is more to that.

Pa: This ain't a thriller movie or some shit. Can one of you complete the scene for me?

He got the entire download from Her. She detailed the entire day about what she had done, why she had to bunk and that she felt like taking a break and so on... Her mom explained her perspective though. Her Pa felt like a judge; no more PM, this time. But he didn't know what the exact expectations or arguments there. She wanted the spy issue to be solved, and Her mom wanted the entire control.

Pa: There is nothing wrong with her bunking, as it's not bunking, TBH. College was closed, and hence she chose to enjoy the day. Our kid deserves such breaks. But, I am not okay with you spying on her.

Mom: I never spied on anyone. In fact, I don't need to. One of my friends went to the movie and saw our kid. So, don't I deserve to know all of her plans? She needs to be more accountable.

Pa: Well, you have a point there. She will be more responsible from now on. You can relax now. He winked at her kid, signaling her to leave from there before Her mom created more ruckus.

Well, this typical drama ended somehow. But, Her mom became more protective since then. She even thought of hiring a spy for a while. Crazy moms!!! She was on it and made sure no other human would be aware of the same; not her husband for sure, at least, after today's judgment. Phew!!! Well, moms do have such potential to pull it off this way or any way. They can be the best spies if the Indian Government would give more benefits to women. Jokes apart, she was that concerned about her kid. She did not care about the hatred she had to go through for the same, but, all about her kid's personal life decisions. A few months passed by exams, studies, and a repeat mode of the same. Nothing new! No bunking for sure, She thought, at least to be cautious of spies. She even made sure that she changed the lock PIN for her desktop. She never wanted Her parents to know about her crushes or anything beyond; especially, not about the staring guy who ended up liking another person. It wasn't a bad thing but for sure, it wasn't a successful one either, to be made public. She always wanted to portray the good side and dump the other side inside Her. If they get to know the chat history and call history, she would have to open up about the chain of her life phases… Why didn't she want to come to the city…? Why didn't she want to talk to anyone for a while…? Why did she study more than required? Also, about her distractions… diversions, and all! Well, it would be a nonstop chain with loaded emotions. It would end up intensifying her mother's protectiveness towards Her. She would get more face packs for Her kid and more brisk durations!! She smartly avoided all of those happenings by a simple screen lock and phone lock. Well, She did get lucky that none of Her mom or Pa have checked her phone/desktop till then. Guilt mode…!!! Arrrggghhh…!

She had her entrance exams for all degree colleges lined up as drunkards stagger in front of bars or pubs. She was all prepared ten days before the first exam. She didn't give much time or importance to the twelfth board exams as they demanded little effort compared to the competitive exams which were the toughest hitherto. But, she made sure there was no compromise, be it any kind of exams as they would affect Her future ranks, if compromised. The first exam was for three hours, and the period, she would never want to forget. One could never forget. The day went as bad as She never wanted a day to go like. It was a mix of feelings of freaking out, weeping, fainting (almost) and a lot more. She could not think for the first 30 minutes; she could not even open her eyes. She felt blank in her head and outside too. There was nothing she could sense or feel. For a moment, she felt like she was stoned. It was that bad. Though she ain't a stoner or smoker, she knew what that does to one. She called her invigilator and asked her for some energy drink as She was about to faint. An immediate medication was given which wasted forty minutes of her exam time. She hated that tutor for calling a doctor instead of giving her the drink that She asked for. She made sure that she used the rest of the time to do Her best. In fact, She did. Then why would she cry or weep?? Well, that's Her!! Welcome to her HAC (Her amazement club). Long time no see. LOL.

She went back home and could not stop crying for the loss of forty minutes. Well, it made sense. She put a lot of effort into this; for more than two years. But, she cried like there was no more hope or options. Her Pa too tried to convince her that there were more exams lined up, and she didn't sit on one exam. In fact, one never knew if she screwed it up. Maybe, she could top this. She always ended up doing this; a weirdo at times though. She gave all her exams and boards too. But her loop never ended. Now, all that she cared about was results. Preparation needed a schedule… exams needed a tensed life… now, the results needed desperacy… a hula hoop. But she made use of the period for her habits, which were waved bye at, for a long time. Horse riding was something, she had been waiting for, and she thoroughly enjoyed it. Now, she got that extra benefit from her trainer. He saw her hoardings in the city and fell for her talent. Fortunately, she could get extra time from him for the habit. Even the celebs waited for him, at times, but not her. See, money can't buy you everything every time. She had that pride in herself and carried an attitude that her effort in studies paid her huge ROI; in simpler terms, good profits. She deserved that diversion; it was what Her Pa believed. Even though she seemed joyful, that was limited to outside. Tadaaa… her results were out after a few days. She could top, but again not all exams. And weirdly, She topped the exam where she fainted (almost). Well, she didn't top but ended up getting a decent rank for the exam, which she felt she nailed. It happens, kid!! Her mom was so happy for Her ranks and achievements, but even happier that she could take her kid to a parlour for body spa sessions and make her look too hot and sexy before she hit the colleges. Hot and sexy in a way that She could get good rishtas, not boyfriends. Well, everyone reading this knows that it can't work that way. Every female ends up having a boyfriend irrespective of looks or concerns. That's how it worked and will work!! To each their own!!!! This fact might get a mini heart attack for Her mom, but nothing could be done TBH.

Her summer vacation kick-started with a set of new responsibilities; to smartly choose a college. In contrast, Her friends had to pray to get, at least one good rank, which meant that they had no options as She had. She planned all strategies in choosing the campus by talking to faculty, professors, seniors, and many other sources. She ended up sitting for hours on her desktop and tablet to do online research on the same. It helped her a lot in filtering the options. She easily found around twelve good options through the results. Well, it was a tough task. But, she was headstrong about not staying at home, this time. She had been dreaming about Btech life for eons; hostel life, independent life, night overs with friends and TV series, activities, and many more. It was evident that She was too tired of her monotonous life hitherto. Though She didn't want to compromise on her future grades or placements, At the same time, She wanted to enjoy a bit of college life, gangs, and camaraderie. Maybe, she thought that She could bunk without her mom spying on her. Little did she know about typical moms… they are more powerful than official spies we have in India. Maybe, moms' talents have crossed borders and reached overseas. One can never underestimate them when it comes to protectiveness towards their kids. Well, she hated being pensive about all those aspects and continued dreaming. One fine day, Her mom tried forcing Her for a spa session. She denied it, not because she didn't want to go but due to Her mom's motive. Now, she is an eighteen-year-old kid and smart enough to know the patterns. The conversation went like this……….

Her: I know your motives and gimmicks, but also try to be smarter from now onwards. Realize your kid's smartness from now. I don't hint you indirectly but directly.

Mom, after coming out of Her shock, replied as…

Mom: Then, you should also know the smartness of your mom; Her concerns; Her motives; Her liking and Her selflessness towards her kid. You should try to know these patterns in a better way. To be precise, think for yourself, at least. I ain't going to gain one per cent of the benefits through the stuff I ask you do. I know you are dark-skinned. I also know you are strong enough to face and cut down racism. But, I don't want anyone to face such scenarios, especially, my kid. It's not that I don't trust your guts; in fact, I do more than your Pa. But, all of these planning is for your future. The world still has racism everywhere. You just have to be smart, play smart and stay smart. Pull it off being that way. Rest is up to you, kid.

She was in awe. She could accept her mom for every jiffy of her given speech and for every spoken word. But, She truly felt that one should not care too much about looks. Spa sessions, face packs, and all could not serve as a hundred percent solution. She didn't mind following the skincare routine, but not that way for sure. Maintaining skin type is entirely different from maintaining complexion. In fact, most of my readers, too, should give it a thought. Even all the beauticians over there should change their diction while conversing with their clients. Apart from these facts, She liked the last ten-fifteen minutes, spending with her mom. It was exciting to see her mom that way. Maybe, she started knowing her mom better. Godspeed!!!

After a few weeks of horse riding, swimming, gymming, and online research, She finally decided to be on her campus. One of the best colleges, one could ever get. She was too happy and overwhelmed as She got into the stream (CSE), she wanted so badly. She even started going for coding classes to ace them at the campus. She always had that balance and pre-planning from an early age. In fact, that's an asset to anyone of that age. Luckily, she carried it for a long period. She hated losing on habits or giving in to things so easily. Her Pa was very excited, but this time, he just couldn't stop boasting about it. He went around telling his friends, relatives, and even some strangers. They also planned to go for an outing as a family after a very social media, so many unread messages were there. Many of her friends, juniors, and seniors congratulated her on getting into an NIT. It was next to impossible for all of them to get into such a reputed one. But instead of thanking them, she ended up sharing her upcoming holiday plan. She could not stop typing, once the conversation started. All of her friends were so J of her (not of her admission into NIT but her trip to Singapore). They could not stop asking about trip plans and all. She had to keep herself sane at this and hence didn't give much details. It's always good to avoid jinxing that way. After a spree of shopping, packing and planning, they were finally three days away from the departure. That was her first flight BTW. She wasn't even sure about the turbulence levels; She researched about it and got to know. She felt a bit nervous after her boarding, but her excitement was the dominating emotion for the rest of the week. The pilot greeted them through the intercom. Safety guidelines were announced and enacted. Then, they were thousands of feet above sea level in a jiffy. But, soon she did realize about her aerophobia due to which she screamed so badly that her parents got embarrassed and made weird faces; as if she stopped there. She even got airsick and felt like vomiting, but luckily she could rush to the restroom before that. For a moment, everyone made weird faces like they were at their peaks of OCD. Little long time. Even She couldn't deny it. It was an International holiday, this time. Thanks to her rich dad and his business ROI. She just could not stop researching the place and its best spots to be visited, food, language, customs, and all that she could. Well, I hate creating this suspense for you people... It was Singapore! Now, you should be able to decode why she was super excited. Yes, Singapore is one of the best places to visit when it comes to punctuality and cleanliness. There is zero percent littering found in the surroundings like roads, open spaces, and public transport. She was the best OCD kid ever, or the most OCD-carrying head. She wanted to shop a lot. She even chatted with so many of her friends. As soon as, she logged in to her did they know that none could beat Her in that aspect.

There, they were roaming and lazing around on Singapore roads. She loved every nook and corner of it. One couldn't find anything that was dusty or littered. There was silence and peace everywhere. The guide was always on time, even if any natural disaster could happen. That showed how important being punctual was to them!! I wish even if thirty percent of our highly populated nation would follow that. The best view spots were visited. I do not prefer mentioning the names and places, as mine is not a book guide to Singapore! Phew! She could not sleep at night due to her over-excitement. She had anxiety issues and many nightmares on the flight journey too. She felt it tough to keep herself in a sane manner. She wanted to gather a lot of info about the nation which her guide had no clue about. He could hardly understand her queries; Those were that deep, maybe intense or maybe senseless. She missed her tablet and desktop which were the only sources for her to search. Her mobile was not recharged for ISD. She wanted a better guide for sure. No luck!! Three days went on roaming, visiting, dancing, and a lot more. But, she wasn't satisfied with it as she wanted to know more about people and customs. She did bore her parents about the same. They realized about the trip long time back where- She ended up sitting in a museum. They were scared if the same scene would repeat. As they were beyond borders and seas, it would be very tough to find her if She got lost. She ain't a kid, but for sure, a nutcase in knowing things. She was too adamant about knowing things there that might end her up getting lost. Hence, Her parents requested the guide for better plans and visits in the next three days. He had to agree and approve it after listening to Her parents as they explained the entire crankiness of Her and Her chronicles to date. He was amazed but scared about what if she ended up going around alone? Hence, he took them to a military camp where she could get all the answers. She was more than thrilled and amazed at the rules the nation had. Every guy had to be part of the army services at least once in their lifetime. There was zero percent robbery recorded in the nation; three percent molesting and rape cases. It was one of the safest nations to live; that's what she believed. They even stayed at the army camp for a day or two. She go most of her answers though her questions, which were not related to the army and their work. She felt that period was the best version of the trip.

In fact, she never wanted to leave after the camp visit. It was a whole different experience for her. But, one thing she hated was to get back to the flight as the arrival had a nightmare. She didn't want to repeat the same. But, she was well aware that it was beyond her control. This time, she took a soda drink before the take-off to avoid air sickness, nausea or all that embarrassing stuff that might happen. It was hundred percent luck; she survived the four hours in a very comfortable manner. But, as soon as She landed, she was happy about getting rid of aerophobia and parallelly sad that the trip ended. But, She knew she had lots of stuff to post and boast about on her social media handles. In fact, she was waiting to get hold of her tablet. She even named it Baby. LOL... Maybe, she felt that, at least, She had *someone* to call that way. Poor singles!!! She jumped and hopped on her mattress; felt happy reaching her room... her space... her area... her thing. The only place, she preferred staying at, for 24/7/365 moments, was her room and the cozy corner she created in her room (with two blue bean bags); one for her bum to rest and the other for her legs. She ain't that tall to need two bags for that; to each her own!! She lazed around the corner for more than a few hours and relaxed. She finally went to her mom and asked her to accompany Her to a body spa parlour. Her mom was in shock but happy that Her kid was finally empathetic towards her. Moms.... moms.... moms.... and their hilarious drama!! They spent a nice day out together, after like eons. Her mom enjoyed it thoroughly and loved every bit of the day spent. They ended up shopping too; eating, playing games and a lot more...! As soon as they reached home, they had to confront everything to the head of the family. Obviously, they had to as he was the only earning person. He made them realize that they were well settled and rich but not that rich to take spa sessions and shopping right after an International trip. She cooled down Her Pa offering French fries and apologized. But, that night changed her a lot. It hit her hard enough that she sat in front of her desktop for hours to search for internships or part-time jobs as she had, at least, five weeks for her campus life to start. No luck though!! She wanted to be financially independent and also lend a hand to her Pa through Her income (if she gets so). That night definitely hit her hard that way. Godspeed !!!

She didn't stop hunting for her part-time job whilst She continued her horse riding classes. She grew her confidence through the same. She felt her skills got uplifted through this habit. Though logically, it doesn't work that way, it worked for Her. A weirdo for a reason...but it's always good to feel that habits change us a lot. She even started stitching, as Her mom loved that habit. Now, as they grew rich enough that they took an overseas trip recently, she stopped stitching and had a tailor (designer- fancy version!!!) to design her clothes and stitch them accordingly. But, She felt the urge to use the machine, started stitching and even sketched different designs to help the former part. Her mom was totally thrilled looking at Her skills. In fact, She rarely did anything creative (according to

Her mom). She imagined herself opening a designer house for her kid, promoting it, designing for celebrities, clicking pictures with them and posting everywhere, gaining more momentum in her kitty party circle…; 100 billion thoughts in a jiffy. Only moms could have such crazy, bizarre imaginative and visualizing powers. But, Her kid was always alive to disrupt her powers. She immediately screamed to make her conscious. Her mom came out of the moment and planned to discuss the same. But…

Her: No ways! Why can't you stop watching idiotic TV shows which get you these crazy thoughts????!!!!

Mom: I suggested you. I never forced things on you.

Her: Ok, thanks! I ain't interested. I will think about the same post my MBA. In fact, I will sponsor you with a designer home if you want one.

Mom: I ain't interested. Just chuck it!

Both of them got irked and left from there. She never wanted to go back to the sewing machine forever. Not because she didn't like it but to avoid Her mom. In fact, she never wanted to start a new habit, at least, in front of Her mom. She suddenly got a ping from her inbox. She saw the toaster notification on her phone and tablet too. She opened the mail and saw her admission details. DOJ, Fee and all typical ones were displayed. It was manifested in an organized manner. She was so, so, so thrilled to start her college, which were in a few days and not weeks. Her hostel life bucket lists would be exhausted in no less than two weeks. She ran to her Pa and mom to explain things. But her mom didn't like it, as she didn't want to stay away from her kid. This time, the residential campus was in another state and not in another district (like in her Grade 1). Only in that aspect, Her dad was with her mom. Even he felt the same, as the only energy ball in the house would be no more in the house, for a while. Of course, he couldn't dare to puke it out as his wife would murder him for such an honest or maybe brutal confession *(Am I, not your energy ball???* would be her version). So he kept it to himself. He had mixed emotions of happiness, sadness, pride, and loneliness. He was more friendly with his kid than with other clients, partners or friends. He hated the home without Her for sure. All of them were attached to each other like a nuclear family. He and his wife knew it would cost a lot this time if they would plan to make frequent visits to her campus. The only option was to fly as they couldn't travel in a bus or train for twenty-two hours.(a li'l rich people maybe). It was Kerala!!! But, She didn't think about any of these as she got the stream she wanted. She started packing as only a few days were left. She planned to meet all her friends, wave goodbyes and disperse. All of her close ones felt emotional, but She was blind to her friends' tears or Her parents' tears. Not in a bad manner, but she was not conscious of that aspect. She was too excited to give it a thought about the former. She planned to spend the last two days at home with her mom. In the end, all that a girl needs is a mom's lap and her head massage. They are the solutions to ninety percent of the youngsters' problems.

The night before leaving, she packed all that had to be packed. She dragged the suitcase outside her room and left them in her drawing-room. To her surprise, She saw a small present placed on the sofa inked with her name on it. It had a set of fictional books; all from her bucket list, which was on a sticky note in her room. Her Pa surprised her that, way, and she couldn't stop weeping as that was the moment when she realized the fact that she was actually leaving. The next morning goodbye was the hardest one. She took the cab to the airport, boarded the flight, saw the land from above, left the city teary-eyed, and said bye in her head. In fact, She was leaving her home alone after eons, and that hit her hard. *It better be worth it, leaving all my best things and going to the hostel.* That's what she told herself. Else she thought that she would drop out and join a college in her city itself.

Chapter- 2

She stepped into the campus with a heavy heart. For the very first time, She missed her mom so much that her tears were out of stock to express the same. It was mid-July and raining heavily. She could not find any help, at least, for the first few minutes. She turned her head many times with her luggage and baggage. At last, She found some cleaners and received help. They had the map of the entire campus in their heads and helped her find the admission office. She took some snacks and finished all the formalities. She was glad that she chose to come a little early to avoid queuing. TBH, she reached the campus a day before and not hours to the reporting time. Her plans might be annoying, but she was smart enough to pull them off well. She reached the hostel and loved the view from her window. It was too good to avoid. She just stared at the rain, trees, and mountains. It was a hilly area. She legit felt that her family deserved a trip to there. Damn…! Finally, She realized her mobile had no network signals, which might have created a ruckus back home. Her mom would be sobbing; her Pa would have tried to contact her at least, hundred times. She just stopped imagining and visualizing things that hurt and immediately rushed down to the warden for an emergency call option. She was provided with a cell phone, through which she called her parents and made them relax. Well, she underrated their emotions. It was worse than how she imagined it to be. Her mom could not utter a word out of tension about what her kid might have gone through. She kept silent, but her husband grabbed the phone and got all the updates like a typical parent who goes like...

When have you reached, kid?

Are all the provisions available?

Admission process timing?

Had food or snacks?

Travel went well, right?

And, is it a co-ed hostel?

Stay safe.

Don't roam without company.

Well, it's a never-ending conversation that way. She gave all answers like an interviewee and dropped the call. Then she rushed to the campus to get an optional sim card. She did not need many requirements from her end except that it should have good network signals for calls and the internet. A basic essential for Gen Z kids though!! Then she tried roaming inside the campus post 4 PM. She was bored as the other kids hadn't arrived yet. She missed home and home food a lot that she called home three-four times in a span of four hours. Her mom wanted to fly to her campus ASAP. But, She denied that. She wanted her parents to visit later, not now. It's too soon, as she wanted to find new friends and faculty, to meet them and to greet them and all. She did not want emotional distractions at that moment. She was very sure that she would be homesick if they came and left. She slept alone in her room after reading a novel of her kind. She loves reading psychological thrillers more than any other genre. She dozed off but went through a rough night, as it was disturbed sleep. She woke up to hunger, late at 2 AM and grabbed some cookies packed by her mom. Soon, she realized she didn't like the food at the hostel, as it was all made using coconut oil. That's the one thing she would kill her cook for. She never preferred coconut oil, as her body was allergic to it. But, she poured the same on her scalp before rinsing Her hair. Finally, after munching, she could sleep fine enough that she woke up to door knocking, but not her alarms. She was so happy to see her roomie outside. There was a huge personality and a hefty one; taller and stronger than Her for sure. It scared her a bit, but she covered it up by smiling. They exchanged hugs and greetings too. Her roomie was lucky enough as She could explain every process of the admission, hostel, SIM options, and what not! Like a guide, she helped her finish the formalities. They became close, but again, not close enough that She could share her OCD habit. In fact, there was one thing, She was scared about her roomie..., and it was if the room would be kept clean or not (it has to be this way). To test the same, She rushed to her snacks box and shared some chocolate and cookies with the her. But, very soon, She realized that she got a mini devil in her room who did not even care about littering. She combed her hair and threw the tangled bunches of hair on the floor. In fact, Her roomie was never seen using the bin at all. She could not breathe or decipher all of that, and it suffocated Her in no less than two hours. She finally puked it out this way...

Her: Well, let me be honest with you. I have OCD.

Roomie: Wow. I love such kids. It helps me a lot as I don't clean my room much. You can do the same. I wouldn't mind at all.

Her: What the...? Are you insane? You keep littering the stuff and expect me to clean 24/7 of your shit. Behave like a grown-up!!

Roomie: Excuse me? I am just vacating the room right away. I will request swap options. In fact, none can bear a freak like you, as a roomie. ATB there!

Her: Blah blah blah...Just leave! And, thanks for vacating.

It was a typical ladies' fight. It ended but not well. She hated her day. She called her mom and explained everything like a director. Her mom suggested staying away from all fights, as she might end up with no friends around. But, She had major OCD issues...Why couldn't anyone grasp that? That's how, She felt TBH. She cleaned her room and took rest. She finally found peace in being alone. She could never give in to OCD for anyone on this planet. But, She would not do any such thing at the risk of hurting others' emotions. It's just that her roomie was a nasty one. The latter was extra baggage for the former. As simple as that! She wished for the entire room, post that scene. She discussed the same with the floor warden followed by denial on the same. She hated her second day for the same and rested for the third day to make Herself feel better. Well, the next morning, She had a hectic day schedule planned and shared by the admissions team. All the students had arrived, occupied rooms, greeted each other, and got ready for the Orientation program ahead. They assembled for the same and got an overview of campus life. They were introduced to their respective branches (streams). She found three-four decent kids and camaraderied them. She was so overwhelmed by the arrival of new roomie that she ended up having a night over with her. They watched TV shows, movies, and had lots of popcorn, which they saved during the snack timings in the mess. They were the best friends on campus. They were from the same stream, section, and project group. They had and maintained a rock-solid friendship anyone could ever have. In fact, half of the campus knew about their bond, which grabbed the attention of seniors. Hence, welcome to the ragging life. They got a notice to meet and greet the seniors one fine day. She got shit scared and reported to the warden about the same as the notice was suspicious. Her roomie or bestie supported her. In fact, all the first years were gossiping about the same. Firstly, seniors were restricted to enter the first years' zone or campus or hostel. Secondly, they should not contact any juniors unless needed for any event help which should be through an official way of communication. But, that notice didn't belong to any of the above. So, it was a clear evident that it was an unofficial way of addressing juniors. Hence, She took a step forward and dared to report about them. Now, she became famous as her name was heard around every nook and corner of the campus. All the students (seniors involved in this) were given a serious penalty and punishment for not being compliant.

She felt so good, and that pride was visible in her walking style, attitude, and whatnot! She felt like a minister with lots of powers. Her bestie was there to support her 24/7/365. She even ended up mentioning all of that to her Pa and not Her mom, as Her mom would mention the same boring lines as how she did in Her ex-roomie's case. He was glad but asked her to be extra careful from then on. He even spent ten minutes with Her bestie. He spoke all those typical lines to be spoken…

Eat properly, kids.

If not, I will parcel the snacks from here.

Have you been avoiding guys? Not that every guy is a good one nowadays.

Do not get into bad habits.

Eat… sleep… study… exercise too.

Stay away from all fights and issues.

Have a good bonding with all the faculty and professors.

Try coming home sometime soon.

Well, She got it through her bestie's expression and yawns that Her Pa was speaking the regular stuff. She grabbed the phone and said goodbye followed by hanging the call. Then, they had a hectic day with loaded workshops and classes. They exchanged their tops or tees, if needed. They never stopped amazing others on campus. After a few weeks, they got their schedule for term exams. They both realized that they had spent many nights watching shows and movies, and had no clue about the classes. She started focusing on her exams and workshops, gave exams and finally decided to take a leave for two-three days; she flew back home. Her bestie could not afford the flight rates and stayed there. She promised to get good snacks and gifts from home. Her mom and Pa were surprised at her arrival, as that was the sole intention of Her. She didn't inform anyone before taking the flight except her warden, as she needed her approval. She was so relaxed. It had been three months, and she realized how much she missed her bean bag, room, desktop, parents and a lot more! Well, parents not being the last, but again not being the first, as they could face time each other. She went to the office with her dad and helped him a bit there. She even cooked good meals for Her parents. She went for a spa session, got a de-tan massage (as the place she stayed was super-hot and humid), a pedicure, and many more. She realized that she spent a lot of time on flights and parlor sessions. But, She wanted all of that for a while as she was super tired of hostel life. She wasn't ready to give in, but she needed the break. Her mom wanted her to stay back, but IRL that couldn't be done. It was a short break for her… she didn't feel like she had enough of it… It was in a jiffy that the past three days went by. She took the flight back to her campus and reached safely. As promised, she took lots of food and a small gift for her bestie. The latter opened the gift and was more than thrilled to see scrunchies. Her bestie loved scrunchies, and hence, She got them for her. The latter had a cute ponytail due to which scrunchies looked even cuter on her hair. They hurried up and went to classes. As usual, it was boring, and they both bunked for the day. They had a decent percentage of attendance so that they could bunk. But, She was on the narrower part of it as she had already missed classes due to Her visit to her place. They went to a cafe nearby and had lots of junk food. She realized that she was running out of money gradually. She wanted to do part-time work to earn bucks. So, she searched online for the same but had hard luck; she couldn't find one. She didn't give in to it though. She decided to work as a teaching assistant to her professors after 'N' number of approvals. She was treated very special by her seniors, to put it in simple terms, She scared them enough. They stopped thinking about ragging Her. That somehow, She got her an army on her side. She never chose to be a leader or some hyped person. She wanted money to go home frequently and help her Pa whenever needed. She wanted things to be simple. But, it was life that chose a different pattern for her. Lots of admiration, Respect, Camaraderie, help and a lot more that She could get right in the first year. It was overwhelming, not for Her but for her bestie. The latter decided to make use of it in her further days to rag juniors. She loved being powerful inside the campus, at least, for a while. But, not in a bad way though. You know, just like a typical bachelor's student's mindset to be strong and powerful inside the campus.

One fine day, She woke up and found a text saying "20K deposited". She was pretty sure Her Pa was rich but wasn't too rich to deposit 20K as pocket money. She was stuck in a maze and clueless what to do. She was aware of fraudsters, cyber-crimes and all kinds of online money bullying that happened. So, she didn't give the text much importance. She went back to her bed and lazed around for a while. She could feel her PMS going bad, but had no option except to leave the room and hit the class. An attendance alert on her head made her do that. She was used to pushing her bestie every morning. In fact, it was a tough task to wake her up. They had their brekkie and ran to class but ended up getting the first row, which any college student would hate or loathe their entire life for. Post her class, she rushed for Her part-time work and to her surprise, it was her professor who deposited the amount. 20K for two months! *What a great work has she done to get so many bucks!* It would be the first impression of any first year if heard about that. She was in the same mind set too, but she never daunted her skills. The next minute after that, she called her Pa and mentioned the same. Her mom could hear the news as the phone was on speaker and grabbed the phone from her husband and greeted Her. She obviously never stopped irking her kid and ended up mentioning "Take care of skin tan", "Make sure no extra tan or other issues, and "Hair fall issues too..." To not sound weird, she added, "Take care and Stay safe." at the end. Her Pa just sighed and cut the call. Maybe, he would have imagined what *his* kid felt like. She took her bestie and few other kids for a beach visit and treated them with lots of snacks and biryani. They were tired of having mess food for sure. Even, her homemade stuff got exhausted very soon. Hostel life was never ending that way. No amount of good food or money could satiate the hostellers. They spent the evening with some beers, roadside junk, and lots of ice cream. They never felt like going back to the prison (hostel), but they were aware of their night curfew timings. It had consequences, like parents receiving calls, semester backs, hostel out, and many other severe ones, if not reached on time. Dating life would have been pathetic in such colleges. They rushed and got the worst bus just to reach on time. She could clearly map the difference between airbus and road buses, but also felt that she should become more adaptable. Fortunately, they reached early by five minutes. They were all super tired and jumped on their beds. She realized that she had to mail a few reports; her part-time work. She knew she couldn't enjoy the money without working.

The next day, she had to miss her class due to her crazy hangover. And the same happened with her roomie and other kids. None of them went to their first class. She was worried about her attendance and rushed to the faculty for a check on the same. She got to know that there was no more bunking, at least for the first year a.k.a two months. Yes, she was going to be a senior in a few months. She was aware of the club events and fests, which were lined up. So, she badly wanted to be extra participative in those, but could not anymore due to her attendance shortage. She applied for a dance club, and writing competition and helped out many seniors in the events and arrangements. Ragging and complaints were long gone shit. None remembered that anymore, even if they have remembered, it was pointless. It's too late that way. Everyone on campus was too excited for the fest launch. It was the most awaited time for any NITC student. She was busy in the same way, she handled events back in school as SPL. All kinds of nostalgia hit her. She forced her parents to attend the event. They couldn't make it due to prior commitments though. She hosted around three-four events with prior advice from seniors and super seniors. Somehow, she became their favorite through her way of handling things. They were left with only one option else to praise her for what she was rather than to hate her. She was that powerful and smart. Fest went well...she managed her classes through proxy methods; she got a few concessions from the administration for conducting events. .Exams were lined up, now, which was a big terror. For her, it was double terror because of both part-time stuffs, and exams. She reached her room, and to her surprise, there was no one while she was expecting her roomie. They had a plan to shop for groceries. She texted her and got seen zoned. She tried calling her many times but ended up with no response. She searched for her throughout the hostel. It was 9 PM which was like the curfew time, and She got super nervous; had no clue. She rushed to the neighbour's rooms and informed them about the same, but found no help there! She ran to the warden and detailed it. There was like a high alert aura everywhere around the campus. The hunting for her roomie started everywhere on the campus. Every student knew that she was missing including the other staff. Her bestie became famous overnight TBH. And, once the warden decided to involve cops in the issue, there was a text received on Her mobile that *she went out with her BF.* She had no clue who that imaginary character was. There was never a single time, she mentioned of him. Despite them being besties for almost a year, She was never informed. She got raged. She informed the warden that her bestie was taking a shower in a different wing, and that she texted Her the same.. Everyone yawned and dispersed. She managed it somehow though she felt she needed not to do it. She ran to her room and pressed her head real hard against the pillow. She was teary-eyed. She was hurt TBH. She always shared everything with her bestie and expected the same from her. She didn't even mind spending her income on her bestie. She threw the pillow once all these thoughts ran in a loop in her head. She waited for the morning so that she could deal with her roomie.

6 AM: She woke up and saw her bestie lying on her bed. She couldn't control her anger. She shouted her name so the latter would wake up. And she woke up frightened.

Roomie: What's wrong with you? Why are you yelling even before I woke up?

Her: To wake you up! Do you realize the way, we searched and hunted for you, yesterday?

Roomie: I know and I apologize that I didn't inform the same.

Her: Only one apology?

Roomie: Ok, egoistic friend! I didn't want anyone to know about my private life. We are just dating; nothing more than that. And, hence, I didn't share the same with you. But, I ain't gonna apologize for this.

Her: How rude?!

Roomie: Are you sure? Because you never cared to inform me about your part-time work. You were the one distancing yourself from everyone and especially me. You could afford the time to party with all of us, but not two minutes from your time to mention the same to me. But have I confessed any of this? Have I ever been rude?

Her: I am sorry.

She was speechless. She didn't know how to answer that. So, she left from there. Her bestie went back to her bed and fell on it. She loved sleeping more than anything; maybe more than the imaginary character (BF). She had her brekkie and left for class without her roomie. She was on a guilt trip. She needed some diversions. She wanted to keep herself occupied. She realized that her exams were near and hence, took them for granted. She was in the library 24/7 and had her meals too, there. She was not literally inside the library, but in the mini canteen in the surroundings. She wasn't strong enough to go back to her room as she didn't want to face Her roomie. She missed her a bit but focused more on her schedule. Little did she know how much her roomie cared about Her. She arrived at the library and took Her back to their room;

actually dragged her forcefully. It was a good patch-up that way. They exchanged hugs and a cheek kiss too. Don't judge! It's fine for girlfriends to kiss on cheeks. They were back and got into combined study mode. Her bestie wasn't that great at scores and ranks. She definitely sought hundred per cent help from Her. They had their schedule planned using day planners and day journals those were stuck on their walls. Too many sticky notes added colors to their room. It attracted many viewers too. Exams... Day 1... Day 2... Day 3... It was done and suited! Yes, that's how it works in B-tech colleges. It was way better than the 11th and 12th Grade boards. It was home time... vacation time, and especially for Her, it was horse riding and swimming time. She missed them badly.

She waved at her bestie the hardest goodbye and left for her city. She was always known to land out of nowhere... she never pre-texted her parents about her arrival or holiday. Her mom gave her a teddy hug and didn't leave for at least a few minutes. She yelled that she couldn't breathe and then her mom had to. It had been more than three months since she came home. So, it made sense for moms to give such irritable hugs. She ran to her Pa and gave him the same hug she got from Her mom. Her mom had all J rolled up in her eyes. She left from there and started cooking. Come what may! Moms always feed us the best when we return after hostel life. She could smell the odour and be so tempted to deposit some fats in her body. She knew her mom cooked the yummiest food which had high calories. She saw her room maintained the way it was when she left the last time. She jumped on her bean bags and relaxed for almost thirty minutes. She dozed off and woke up to her mom's yelling. *Food ready. Served hot. Come fast.* She ran to grab all of them and had super fun enjoying the meal. She relished them. She took a nap and sat on her desktop for hours. Suddenly, she sees a text from her flashback Staring Guy; her Past Crush. She had a smile on her face and opened the message with lots of excitement. Maybe it was no more her past crush; she still had it like one per cent for him. She was a sulk pot that way. She couldn't move on hundred percent forever. And the conversation went like…….

Her: Hey. How are you? Long time.

Him: Don't fake it, too much. You never care to text me except when I start the convo.

Her: I was caught up with my first year. It was hectic and all. You know!

Him: Yeah sure. Fake-star!

She smirked because he would not be able to see it. She blushed. She had those lonely moments flee for a while. She always felt that way when he texted Her. OG girl. Maybe that was the reason, She couldn't move on yet.

Him: Are you there? Reply!!!

Her: I am reading our previous texts.

Him: Me too.

For a moment she was shocked. Despite all of the girly moments, She realized that he was dating someone else. But, She felt the connection was weird. *I mean why would he text out of nowhere? He has a girl. Maybe he likes me as a good friend to share stuff and all. Of course, why not? Even my bestie at campus did the same. She loved my company despite not sharing about her BF.* She got distracted due to many toaster notifications sounds…..

Him: Hello?? Reply!!! Are you for real?

Like twenty times in three minutes.

Her: Let me make it clear to you that this is all weird. If you have your girl and text me this way, I might judge you as a despo.

Him: What? I thought we were close enough to pull it off this way. I ain't flirting or wooing you here. In fact, I don't have a girl, anymore.

Her: Hence proved.

Him: WTF?! Do you really feel like I am here for a rebound or flirting?

Her: IDK....Bye

Him: Wait...! I didn't text you all these days, as I deactivated all of my social media handles. I wanted to be isolated and I was. But, I thought of meeting you as I am in your city. I want a good company like yours. I ain't here to date you or whatsoever you think like.

She felt that both were excited and depressed after seeing his last text. The former was due to *him not dating anyone* and the latter part due to *him not having it for her.* She was in a maze with all the pings, leftover emotions for him, and a lot more!

After a few minutes, she cared enough to reply, or else too many texts might pop up. Impatient guy friends sucked at times.

Her: You need not explain all of this. You can date whoever you want. But I am not ready to meet you yet. I have caught up on stuff at home.

Him: Lol. Bye.

Her: ?!!

Damn. She was seen zoned. She hated it the most out of all possible social media blunders. She got into "No Fucks" mode from now on, especially towards him. She ran to her Pa who was about to leave for some biz meeting. She wanted to accompany him; the best diversion one could get post a debate. She wore biz formals and a blazer. TBH, She was overdressed. Her Pa wasn't a billionaire or some biz magnate yet. Her Pa felt the same.

Pa: What are you dressed for?

Her: Meeting!

Pa: Do you not see what I am wearing? Do you want me to feel daunted now? Go change, girl.

Her: Fin-eeeeeeee!!!!!

She had to break the word to induce some anger and irritation. She felt *Why would all guys behave weird?* She changed in a jiffy and left with her pa. In the meeting, all of them wore biz formals and she hated her Pa for asking her to change. Then, she could decipher the logic that her Pa was underdressed, and that was the only issue for him;

nothing else. Man Ego! She felt like she lived in an aura of Man Ego. She somehow attended the meeting, but was desperate to confess to her Pa about it. Once they reached…

Her: What was wrong with me wearing the blazer?

Pa: Nothing. I didn't want to flaunt much. They are our investors and hence they can pull it off that way.

She was shocked as he answered about it, even before, she could compare it with them. She had to leave tight-lipped, as she mistook her Pa. She soon realized that the Staring Guy debate has affected her a lot. Maybe, she liked him way too much. That's how she felt, and she was scared of the same. She hated being emotionally dependent. She ran to her desktop and texted him. For the very first time…! She never initiated the conversation unless there was an SOS!

Him: Finally.

Her: I need to tell you something.

Him: Shoot!

Her: I have been dating a guy, and he doesn't like me texting you.

Him: What?

Her: Yeah. IKR. Too much.

Him: Kewl. TTYL.

Her: Okay.

That's how girls get things done at times; can't agree more. She had to pull off that step, as she realized she was INTO him!!! No reasons and no logic! She still had it for him and only Him!!!

Him: There?

Her: Yes? Thought you said TTYL.

Him: I don't like you dating him.

Her: What? Why?

Him: Because you have to break up with him. Right now!

Her: For? Are you for real at all?

Him: Because I broke up with mine for You!! Dumbass.

She was in awe. She jumped. She yelled but not that loud to drag her parents into the room. But, she went back to "Attitude Mode". She enjoyed that pulling leg concept of Hers.

Her: As in?

Him: Really?

Her: Yeah. Tell me.

Him: I want you. Like a good friend. Bestie. Partner. Everything. Every moment. I realized it very late. I wanted to tell you all of this on your face. But you denied meeting me. Meh.

She was teary-eyed as she got answers to many of the questions she had for the past few years. She had many mocking her for OG love blah blah… many more. But, she didn't give in to him. She definitely didn't confess but dumped every emotion related to Him inside her. She felt the best and was so happy that she yelled, but this time, her mom banged the door.

Mom: What happened?

Her: A video game I won! After many years. You can go. Don't worry.

A brilliant liar. Soon, she realized that he deserved a ping now.

Her: Let's meet and talk.

Him: Sure. When and where?

Her: I will let you know. Give me a while. It's too much to decipher, and it takes time for me to think it out.

Him: Sure. BYE. Tc!

Girls being girls!

She could sense inner peace in her for a while. She also doubted if she was too open through her last text. She wasn't sure. She was scared and felt dubious about it. *Have I given him a hint through my last text? Loosening threads?* But, she rested peacefully the entire night. She didn't care to wake up for horse riding. TBH, She woke up at 12 PM. She rushed to her mom yelling...

Her: Why haven't you woken me up?

Mom: Really? You bolted your door from inside. Do you expect me to do some magical shit to end up there?

Her: You should have yelled or called me or something a mom would do.

Mom: WOW!! Now, go get the hell out of my kitchen and get some Listerine.

Even she could smell her shit from her mouth. She ran to wash her mouth and later came for a brekkie. Her mom made her realize that it was noon and not time for brekkie. She had lunch and hated Herself for a while and hence bunked horse riding, didn't freshen up and ended up in the kitchen, compromising on her OCD and hygiene levels a lot more! That was exactly what she was scared of; to get into a relationship. *Giving In To Oneself Easily.* Maybe, that's also one of the reasons that she couldn't date anyone hitherto. She decided not to text him back for a while and continued with her online courses and other habits. She had a few weeks left to go back to her campus. This time, it's going to be different at the campus as she would be a Senior. Though she ain't cool enough to rag and stuff, at least, she would not need to follow her seniors. She always appreciated such a life. She even decided not to go out much as long as he stays in the city. Not sure if. he might turn up anywhere. She had a blend of guilt and anger. A few weeks passed by similarly where she went to her morning classes, online courses, biz meetings, eating a lot, burning the fats, and sleeping; but no desktop or social media for a while.

One fine day, Her mom got her to go at the maximum she could.

Mom: I will accompany you this time to college. Nothing doing!

Her: What? Why? How? No... I want to go alone. Let me be this way.

Mom: Stop your Wh's, and I am coming. I told your dad. In fact, he couldn't agree more.

Her: Just stop being this irritable. You can come after I reach. In fact, both of you can come.

Mom: Why are you so worried? Are you dating someone, and is your partner accompanying you? Is your partner from your college or city? School friend? Since when has this been going on?

Her: What the...?! Why do you always have to behave this way?

She got so irked that she left from there, started her packing and booked her ticket Herself. In the next two days, She was going to leave. She didn't inform her mom. Her Pa was on the same page as her though. He agreed to come once she reached her college. He had no clue about the conversation they had (regarding BF and all). She took the early morning flight and landed safely. Her mom woke up to see Her vacated room. She was in shock and was pissed more than ever.

Wife: Where is our kid?

Husband: She left early in the morning, I suppose. Maybe she didn't want to disturb our sleep.

Wife: As in?

Husband: She mentioned this two days ago. I thought you were informed about the same.

Wife: chuck it!

She detailed the conversation they had and the fight too to her husband. He was confused. He didn't get a jack shit what his wife explained but blindly nodded. The only way he could calm her down was by booking the flights. He did the same and shared the news with Her. He called up his kid and mentioned that they both would be arriving next week. She couldn't deny it this time. She said fine and hung up the call. She reached the campus and met her bestie and all the other kids. She realized that she missed the aura quite a bit. Once she reached her room...

Bestie: Long time, right?

Her: Yeah. I missed the room too.

Bestie: How is your new BF?

Her: What? Why is everyone giving me these weird shocks? My mom and then you! What's wrong with this world?

For a moment, she realized how her bestie even knew about him. She turned to her and asked her the truth.

Bestie: He texted me a few days back. He was tensed that you didn't reply. Or maybe you weren't online. I don't know the exact reason. But, he seemed too worried for me to ignore. Now, you tell me why have you hid this?

Her: Wait. wtf... How does he know you? Tell me, what all happened from the start.

Bestie: He saw us in some posts on your social media long back and sent me a request to know your well-being.

Her: OMG... Is he into me? I feel guilty, now.

Bestie: Stop this drama, and now, you tell me what all happened!!!! FOMO...!!

She had to explain her crush days... missing him days... staring at him days... attitude replies... the last convo they had... like every detail how an interviewee could explain to an interviewer. She was too good at it. But, all that while, her bestie could sense the love She had for him. Gave her a huge teddy hug and kissed her on the cheeks. She was so happy for Her. She ran to her tablet. logged in to her account and messaged him...

Her: Hey....I Love You. That's it. Bye.

Him: Not anymore. (with a set of sad emojis)

Her: I am sorry that I ignored you for a bit. But, I do have my own reasons. It's not like I got someone else to date. Or, whatever other typical thought that might hit your head.

Him: You could have texted me, at least, once before you left the city.

Her: I said I had my reasons, and I genuinely feel bad for that. But, how do you know that I left? My bad! You have your spies!

Him: I had to spy on you for 1000 reasons!

Her: I wish I could meet you and explain things.

Him: You can still do it

Her: What?????

Him: I will be coming *soon.*

She had no memory issues and hence could remember her Pa "We will be arriving *soon*". She was scared that these two 'Soons' might collide.

Her: When? Date? Time?

Him: Someone seems too excited and desperate.

Her: You wish. Don't act smart. Just tell me right now.

Him: Coming weekend.

Her: Thank God! Different weekends.

Him: What? Are you double dating?

Her: Very funnyyyyy. Bye. Waiting for you.

Him: Tc! See you soon.

She went back to her bestie, gave a huge tight hug and thanked her; no reasons, but just thanks and hugs. Her bestie too didn't care enough to ask her the reasons to hug and all other stuff. She could sense Her feelings and vibes. All Love vibes! They headed to their campus and were all excited to meet and scare juniors. They could see new things around like a new canteen, a new grocery store and many other developments around. She was so thrilled to explore all the stalls and chill a bit. They ended up bunking. Sometimes, we can't avoid bunking and the reason is the campus itself. Too many things shall be attractive to lessen the value of the classes and studies. She was counting on every moment to meet him, not her parents for sure. Especially, her mom after the bad conversation and fight, they had before she left home. She missed her Pa a bit, but her priority was Him for a while. She didn't mind changing her choices this time, as she didn't want to hurt him anymore. She wanted to be extra careful before taking such a stupid decision like before. *Giving in to him for habits.* She understood that it's all about balancing emotions, which keeps one away from avoiding and other shit.

Weekend arrived. He was there. She woke up and rushed to take a shower. It was 6 AM. She was not sure why such an early shower though. Her bestie felt the same. She went online and waited for his text. There was none. She got pissed. Raged. Irked. She didn't feel anything like a girl would feel right before her first date. Poor guy… dead!!!

At 10 AM….

Him: Hey. I am here. Sorry. Got late.

Her: Hmmm

Him: Stop doing this drama now. Come down.

Her: Wait for 10. I am having my brekkie.

She was doing nothing except waiting for his text. But, she lied; no need to mention why.

She wore the best attire she could fit in. She tried to slay it a bit with her bum. She felt her torso was perfect and way better than many girls'. She wanted to look hot as he was a white champ, taller and hotter. She didn't want to look like an idiot. Ugh!!!

They meet at a posh cafe, staring at each other. No words. Silence. Too much turning the heads to avoid eye contact. Null ice breakers. Awkwardness at its peaks. She hated it more than any other hurdles or adversities she went through.

Her: So…. What else?

Him: You are so hot and cute together. How?

Her: What? I am blushing at that. But thanks for your concern and all. Though I loathe spying and shit, this is a better way of spying. So…

She immediately could recollect the moment when she hated her mom for spying on her movie and bunk shit. She felt a bit guilty. But, She got distracted immediately.

Him: Well, it's fine. I like the bond we had for years amidst gaps, breaks blah blah. It's just the openness we maintain between us, and since then, I wanted to date you. And, trust me, you are in no way a rebound for me. If I am desperate I could have easily…

He paused at her glare, and She felt the moment weird.

Her: As in?

Him: Oops. Sorry. Not that way.

Her: I get it. Relax.

They ordered food and had it like never-had-food-for-years kids. They used that time to save some awkwardness. They did stare at each other once in a while, but she was more into food for sure. They clicked some pictures. She warned him not to post them on any social media handles. He had to agree as if he had any option left. They exchanged hugs, and lots of conversation, hit the beach, and relaxed for a while. they had to leave once she realized about her curfew timings, scary warden, calling parents about their kid missing, cops searching and all other drama that could happen. She reached on time and waved at him. It wasn't a hard goodbye, as they planned to meet the next day. Thanks to the weekends, which happen in pairs rather than alone; sucks to have only a single day off. Her phone distracted her due to many missed calls and toaster notifications. It was Her mom and Pa. There were seen zoned messages which she didn't care enough to reply to. But, as soon as, he left, She realized Her mom's anger and Pa's concern. *Guilt. Sucks.* She texted back that she was busy and would call back later. She rushed to her room and hugged her bestie; too much love and nastiness. She was just blushing for hours, smiling at their pics, remembering the moments spent with him, and more. Her bestie got each and every detail from Her. Girl besties rock it, that way. They made sure nothing would be missed out when gossiping. She went on like ….

Her: Dude! It was my first date; so much showering of love, smirks, and blushing happened. I had no clue how to drive him. I mean he was already driven towards me. He took really good care of me. We spoke a lot and about a lot. We bitched about our childhood friends a bit. But, we miss them for sure. I just love this phase. I am so J of you that you got it way before me.

Bestie: I can see all of that (smirks). Well, just be careful as you never know. We broke up recently due to many stupid issues. I don't want you to repeat blunders like me.

She realized her bestie deserved a snuggle and hugs post that talk. But, she was way too diverted for that to happen. Guilt again. Sucks. She ran to her and gave her warmth through hugs and a kiss on the cheek; a bit of fakeness there. But, it ain't bad that she had to fake it, as she didn't want her thunder to be stolen in any other way. She called her Pa….

Mom: Why can't you take calls or reply to our texts?

Her: Why can't you just pick your own phone and not dad's?

She still didn't forget the bad conversation they had right before leaving home.

Pa: Hello girl. Busy kid? Why don't you just drop a text?

Her: I was busy, and I am sorry. *Lies...too many lies... guilt.. sucks...*

Post the call, she hated all the lies and guilt trips hitting her. She felt that it was too much to take in or digest. But, this time, she was sure not to make any blunders like ignoring him and stuff due to weird reasons. She slept early thinking of all these except her studies. For a moment, she forgot her classes and schedules for the coming week. *It was Sunday - no classes day, second date day, too much happiness loaded day, memories-to-be-created day.... Many more!!!* She met him outside the campus, but this time, he was with his luggage, which reminded Her of his departure the same day. She hated it. But, She had to accept the fact and enjoy the rest of the day. They went for a movie date and had no clue about it as they wanted some privacy to kiss and ended up there. Just a peck though. He dropped her after the movie and flew back to his city. Her city. She missed him even before she reached the campus. He gifted her his jacket to snuggle in whenever she wanted to. It was a posh one though. She loved brands... so, it made sense. She even wore it to her class whenever there was a rough climate. She would have worn it even if it was hot enough TBH; sulk pot, that way. Her practical exams were approaching, and she was clueless what to read. But her bestie was good at them, this time; perks of staying single. Post-breakup life has a different vibe altogether. It was a reverse situation that happened this time. She went to her bestie for doubts. She even went to others for schedules. Everyone got amazed. In fact, few felt bad about Her. She was way better when she was single. That's how everyone on campus felt except her bestie. Maybe, even she felt the same, but was happy for Her. She opted for balance in her life. *High time. No more imbalances. No more weird stares from my friends.* She wanted to top her semester this time too and worked her tails off for that. She texted him once in a while and left the mobile in the room to avoid distractions during class. But, She made sure he was informed of that, unlike the last time where the complete ghosting happened as she was scared of **This Compromising** concept. He respected her decision though. Rare breed. True man. Her exams approached closer, and she was 24/7 in the library or faculty rooms. She didn't care about her club meetings or events. It was just to crack a pointer and a decent job, for which she entered this campus. She was headstrong that way. Finally, she gave her exams, relaxed, and decided to meet him. But, he got busy now. He had his exams a bit later. So, they couldn't meet and that went on for three months. *Hard… Hard… hate it, but let me accept it. I have been born with over-maturity for a reason. I shouldn't get affected by this. Stay there.*

Her routine life went with lots of texting, calling, studies, and exams, but she missed her parents, home, her favorite corner of the house, and her city. Her parents who planned to visit her campus couldn't make it because of the busy schedule her Pahad. Her mom was ready to travel alone though, to meet her kid, but was denied by the same kid. She felt it too much to have just her mom around without Pa. She was still pissed at her mom, which happened a few months ago. At times, having good memory skills suck. It just reminds us of all the stuff, whether it is good or bad! But, one fine morning, her Pa called her saying they were at the airport. She had no clue. That's how we mention things as Surprises!! Well, her Pa was a pro at them. His schedule might irk Her a bit, as many plans get cancelled, but he never compromises to surprise, like compensation for the cancelled plans. They reached the campus. She jumped on her Pa and gave a side eye to her mom; but gave a side hug too as She didn't want to seem rude. All were teary-eyed for the moment. Her eyesight got blurred for a while due to the same. She wiped Her tears before anyone could observe Her. She hated to be emotional that way. The campus had quarters for parents' visits. So, she accompanied them and asked them to rest for a while. It was midweek, and she had lots of submissions ahead. She felt it worse to have such tight deadlines, and that too when her parents were there. It was their first visit. She didn't want to end up cornering them.

The next day, they went for an outing and spent every second with their kid in the best way they could. They visited her classroom, CSE block, hostel, rooms, friends, and the surroundings. They had lot of food, watched the movie and beaches. It was like the hundredth time for Her; she did the same with her friends, with her bestie and with her BF; obviously, She didn't kiss anyone except her BF. But, it gave her a missing feel as he wasn't there this time. His jacket was there though...like always... always to keep her away from such feelings. They went for boating before they could wave goodbyes to each other. They had to leave as Her Pa was such biz person who was always busy, but never wore a blazer for meetings. Weird. She dropped them off at the airport and gave a tight hug to her mom. She shed all the tears she saved for the past few months. She reached her campus safely and called him.

Her: Sorry. I couldn't text or call you. I got busy. Are you done with your exams and all submissions?

Him: Yes dear. You need not feel that way. I have seen your Insta posts. Relax.

Her: Why can't you come?

Him: It has been a long time. Even I feel that way. But, I am out of my pocket money. Sorry!

Her: I get that. No worries. I will try coming home soon. We can meet.

She felt bad about it and started doing her part-time work again to meet him. A few months passed by with her busy schedules, due to which things got roughened between them. She couldn't text, and he couldn't wait; a typical rough patch. But, they stuck to the "No Moving On" concept. It was an unsaid break between them. A bit of ghosting hit them, but none moved on. They couldn't call each other for a few fortnights, but none moved on. A rough patch was placed due to their tight schedules, and nothing beyond that. She was busy with the targets of cracking pointers in her upcoming exams and earning pocket money through her work. She even stopped talking to her bestie due to tiredness. She used to come back and fell on the bed, then woke up and left. Only these moments were spent with her bestie, but minimal interactions though. The same was with her parents. She hardly texted or called them. The final exams approached; she was a bit scared and nervous. Those were the deciding factors for Her to get a good internship in the upcoming year. As soon as she gave her exams, she took the next flight to Her city. That was the first time, she wanted a third person more than her parents or her room. It was Him. She met him at the airport and they hugged so badly that half of the passengers forgot their flight timings and ended up watching them. They cried, hugged, couldn't kiss though, they soothed each other. She felt all of it so good and later left for home. Her mom, as usual, had lots of food on the dining table served. Yummy and hot. She was on her mobile all the time while eating. Her mom surely tried to distract her, but nothing worked. She wanted to compensate for all those days when she couldn't text him. So, she was stuck to her phone. She even realized that nothing like ghosting, not texting or calling for so many weeks could break them apart. They met every two days and slowly met every day which in turn changed to twice a day. She got attached to him. So was he. They shared every detail with each other. They even planned for MBA in the future, to take it up together. Her mom definitely didn't give up on her spying skills. She was sure that there was something shady, but not sure what exactly her kid was into. She didn't want to end up fighting like before, which went on for months. They went for horse riding classes together, as She could spend her pocket money on him. Of course, he couldn't afford it. She was sure that she would end up getting caught by her parents someday but stayed away from such negative thoughts. She enjoyed all the present moments with him in the best way before she could leave for her campus.

Summer vacation couldn't get better than what she was going through. She attained an internship at a small firm which generally is earned by students post the third year. Thanks to Her extra-smart skills! The best part of her relationship was exactly that; he never saw her as some abnormal or extremely talented bum. She enjoyed that the most as her childhood always had HAC alive. It wasn't easy for her to decipher others' comments or her parents hiding her skills to avoid criticism. He opened up such a beautiful path for her. She imagined him as her life partner, biz partner, husband and everything. Sulk Pot! Ugh...! But, She never dared to puke it in front of him. She was a bit scared of that way and maybe egoistic. She wanted that to be initiated from his end, for sure. Every day, she went to work for just four hours, but lied about it at home. She spent around nine hours outside the home, which was tallied after spending five hours with Him. They went to movies and cafes. They boozed, chilled, and relaxed. She never wanted to go back to her campus, not because she doesn't like the kids there, but now her priorities changed. She could feel the balance in her life that she built herself; Him... Her habits... and Her work...He supported her every moment and in every way which he could. She once in a while texted her bestie and gave all the gossip about her dating life. She wasn't much of a text person TBH, but chose it to avoid the distance between Her and Him. She got used to texting only for him and his texts. She felt everything going seamless but also was scared of getting it jinxed. It's just the human tendency, that way. Things went so well that they had to end up something bad. That's exactly how she felt. Weekends were hard though as she couldn't spend much time with him; a maximum of three hours. In a few weeks, she had to fly back to her campus. She knew it's going to be bad and worse in fact. Once you get attached to a human, then leaving them for a while sucks. Sucks in every way! Leaving the city, parents, and home for the first time felt better. She cried and boarded the flight, saying bye to romance… bye to him… bye to all the blabbing… and Bye to everything for a while.

Once, she reached the campus, this time, it was more than being a senior.. She could get more privacy as she got a single room, attached washrooms, mini kitchen and co-ed hostels. In every way, hostel life was made better for Her, but not for him. His insecurities increased due to that. As she had a set of good guy friends back at campus, they all were most of the time hanging out in her room. Of course, there were female friends too. But, at the end, only black dots on the white paper will be seen. Thanks to typical BFs! He tried to confess the same but never found scope. He started texting her bestie about it. He was scared more than feeling inferior. This creates issues only if it crosses a few boundaries. One day, they ended up fighting on the same....

Him: Hey. Sup.

Her: Partying in my room. Enjoying it after a long time with them. Enjoying this phase... It's new as I was always stuck with work and all. Sup.

Him: Hmm

Her: ??

Him: Bye.

Her: Fine? Wanna talk?

Him: Think you are busy. Carry on. TTYL

Her: Kewl. Bye

Him: Ohhh...Hmm.

Her: What's wrong with you?

He immediately calls her on video mode. As soon as she took the call, she switched the cam mode to rear from front mode. He was shocked and felt guilty. It was a normal party with lots of girls and a few guys. All of them were dancing. It wasn't even close to forty per cent of the visuals, he imagined. Jeez!! Guys are guys! He then apologized to Her for all the insecurities he had and for that he couldn't share with Her. She smirked and hung up the phone. It's good to date such smart-ass girls, at times because empathy is always at hundred per cent levels and sometimes, beyond that too. She wasn't okay with his doubts but definitely understood his inferiority feelings and solved them in the best way she could. Her bestie knew all these patterns and texted him back….

Bestie: Clear?

Him: I never wanted to doubt her, but this distance relationship sucks dude.

Bestie: She is a real rare breed, duh. Bye

Him: IKR. Lucky me, but the stupid me! Bye

She had the best people around, though it was a limited circle. Quality matters more than quantity though. Few friends but a good support system! All of them had her back for sure. She deserved to be cast in some fairy tale movie for that reason. It's rare that our friends aren't J of us but push for us. Her bestie too deserved an award for that. She always pushed Her for stuff that changed Her life that making her realize Her mistakes, Her Bf issues, or Her life patterns; in many ways her bestie had her back. It was a fairy tale for sure. He planned to meet his girl very soon, but only Her bestie knew it.

Sssssurprise was coming; not sure if it was out of love or insecurities. Alert mode was on! Well, he missed her for sure. But, She didn't get much time to spend with him, as she had major projects incoming. The third year ain't easy, and that too CSE... it will make you work your tails off come what may. Coding... Submissions... Labs, and tight deadlines. In fact, it's like a collection of all the worst things in one's B-tech life. She had major hair fall issues and visualized her mom being there. She would have been like, *"Let's go, see a doctor... Let's go for parlour sessions... No more good rishtas! How will anyone marry you?"* The entire loop would be coming. She just got distracted and felt the best way to avoid hair fall was to get rid of hair a.k.a getting a haircut.

One day, She received a text from him ...

Him: Woke up? Ready?

Her: As in?

Him: To tour your campus?

Her: Whatttt??!!

Him: Yes.

Her: Seriously! Are you here??!!

Him: Obvio…. Come down! I am at the center campus *(the main part of the admin block)*

Her: How did they allow you in? Why wouldn't you tell me this before? I have oiled hair…I need to wash my hair… *(Girls can do anything except step out in oiled hair)*

Him: Will you stop investigating this and come here?!

Her: Oops… Sorry babe… Coming in 15 minutes.

She rushed to the restroom, washed her hair, brushed them, changed, and then blow-dried hair. All Her makes-her-look-hot clothes were sent for laundry. She ended up wearing her bestie's clothes which weren't bad on Her. She forgot to change her chappal and ended up meeting Him with her bath-wear slippers. They weren't bad though but definitely not the ones for a date. They both had been on enough dates by then. So, she didn't care much even after realizing that She wore slippers. He couldn't stop smirking looking at her… dripping hair… short hair… weird chinos… Basically, he mocked her indirectly.

Her: Stop!

Him: Tough to stop

Her: Get lost. *And, she was about to leave*

Him: Sorry... Wait!

Her: Surprises suck at times! Hence proved.

Him: IDC how you look, just come. Let's leave

Her: Where?

Him: Surprises don't suck... Let me prove it now

Her: LOL. Ok.

He took Her to a nearby hill station which was like forty km away from her campus. The entire drive was a romantic one with climate, music, warmth inside their shawls. But, She was a weirdo as she was stuck with her laptop. She worked 24/7 on her laptop due to tight deadlines. He got irked and tried to snatch it from Her. Oops... Girls hate snatching their stuff for sure.

Her: What even?

Him: Have I come this long to watch you doing this?

Her: IDK. But, I have loads of work.

Him: Hmm

Her: I am sorry but try to get it. Stop sulking. I am right here. You can stare at me… Talk to me… I will respond, but I can't leave my work.

Him: kewl. Sorry. Even though I had many submissions, I am here, right?

Her: Guilt tripping me? *She gave that glare and stare.*

Him: OMG. Can you stop? I am just asking for some time from your end.

Her: I will. But, what's wrong if I work parallelly?

Him: kewl Carry on. I came here for no fucking reason.

Her: What? Are you for real?

No more replies. It was silent and awkward. He felt awful. They both were teary-eyed. She hated it and wanted to end the fight. She hugged him by side and apologized. They were sorted that way. Their fights didn't go beyond a day even in distance mode then it wouldn't make sense for them not to talk for even a few hours when they were beside each other. Cute! They reached the place. She could see a beautiful resort booking done by him. She couldn't stop giving him a quick peck and jumped out of the car. She didn't care about his expenses, and all. She felt that the break was much needed. It was beautiful scenery. Obviously, Kerala is known for the same. It had a play area with a see-saw and other kids' stuff outside the porch. It had a menu that included her city's cuisine. She was more than overwhelmed. She forgot her deadlines in a jiffy. Her phone rang and gave her a distraction. Who else can call her now? Mom!! Ugh..! It is so weird they end up calling only when we are with BFs... like some fucking telepathy! She didn't take it and texted her, *Busy...TTYL*. They had a maid, cook, and a driver at the resort. Now, it hit her about the money spent... She had to ask him.

Her: How??!

Him: What how?!

Her: How did you manage all these?

Him: Do you think I can't afford this?

Her: Seriously?

Him: I was kidding. Even I know how to pull it off through part-time work, baby. This is my first earning, and hence thought of spending it for you.

Her: Not bad. Love you.

She gave him a teddy hug and a tight one like her mom. Then, she gave him more pecks as she truly got amazed. They rushed to their room and snuggled into each other. She felt so good that she didn't want to go back to her hostel. The food, work, and campus all bored her. *It has been three years… same buildings, same people, same faculty, same CSE block.* What not! They had a meal and watched TV for a while. She felt every moment so romantic that her visualizations went uphill. She couldn't stop thinking about her future, biz, marriage, kids and every minute with him. She wanted to stop imagining stuff but it was tough; inevitable. In fact, all of us go through this, especially in emotional attachments. Though it's dangerous, it's also inevitable. Then, they went for a drive to explore more, visited every scenery and viewpoint they could. Once they reached the room, Her work mode was on. She realized her work stuff was pending, shit! She switched on her laptop and started Coding like a pro. Well, he tried to interrupt Her, but he knew he would fail at that. They would just end up arguing. Loop would go on. So, he dozed off. She was smart that way. Firstly, she satiated his expectations by roaming with him and then sat for her work. Now, even he couldn't deny or complain. Epic!

The next morning, they woke up with a brekkie in bed. She felt like a queen in the resort. Their services and hospitality drove Her crazy. She admired every moment with parallel thoughts of hostel life which ran in her head; mess food, damped hair on washroom walls, untidy common areas... Ugh... It's tougher for OCD folks to survive hostels! He fed her the food and took her to the balcony. The view was so good that it just demanded you to get addicted; a true cynosure. They watched some TV shows and he saw her dark circles....

Him: What's wrong with your under-eye spots?

Her: Slept at 4 AM. Work!

Him: OMG! How much do you work?!

Her: Definitely more than you.

They laughed at each other and started packing. She hated it though. None would prefer packing and going back to hell. In fact, every holiday sucks when it's packing to head back to the origin. He drove her back to the campus, left her and returned the car to the service providers. Then, he denied Her accompanying him to the airport and flew back to his place. He stared at the landscape below the plane at some thousands of feet above and was teary-eyed. He didn't want her to come as they both would be emotional about it. Tough facts! She reached and all her friends wanted the gossip. They had been on her Instagram 24/7 to see her feed. Well, he posted more than Her TBH for the past two days. She detailed everything as usual by organizing a party in her single room. It sounded fancy to say Our Own Place in the third year. That's the only part that she loved about her hostel. If not neatness, at least, a bit of privacy!

She recalled her parents after two days. Shit…! Guilt hit harder that way. She called and spoke with them for an hour just to make sure they didn't complain anymore about the last two days… *no calls… no messages… are you dating?* Especially, Her mom! Then, she went to her classes and did the submissions. That wasn't expected from her batchmates as she was on her Love trip… that's how they renamed the trip The entire college gossiped about her trip with her BF. Her competitors felt happy as she won't be a competition anymore. Little did they know that she slept at 4 am working her tails off to meet the tight deadlines. She got good grades too for the submission. Post that, she hit the lab. She loved coding and missed it a bit. Who would want to go and hit the lab to code right after a trip and that too with a BF? That's her. Welcome to Her world! She never wanted to forget the actual Her and Herself. A few got inspired by her way of balancing; a few were confused and a few didn't care at all.

Her bestie was Her biggest fan (in that aspect). This time, for summer vacation, she was sure there was just an internship that was going to be in her daily journal. Nothing beyond. *Well, a tad bit of romance at times ain't harmful.* She had internship interviews at campus…most of them were MNCs. She was sure she would crack it, come what may. She prepared by forgetting the world around her for a few weeks; even her BF. Well, they were in a state where they can understand each other that way. She completely ghosted her social media friends. She woke up and prepared, did coding practice, ate, bathe and slept. Her parents had to call her bestie to know her well-being, as She was no longer using her mobile, at least, for a while. D day arrived; her most awaited MNC PI day was there. She was nervous the most hitherto. She had given her GD, promoted to PI round 1… round 2… final HR round slot was announced, but got shifted to the next day due to panelists. She hated to wait and decided not to go back to the hostel. She remained at the campus itself; practiced, slept, ate and everything on the campus itself. She was scared to go back as the wait might disrupt Her for whatsoever reason. The next day arrived. She was in the same formals as she couldn't change, but got freshened up using the restroom on campus and gave her best. The final results were out but Her name wasn't there. She ran to her room and locked herself in, called her Pa and explained the entire scenario. She realized that she never got that emotional. She booked a flight and went home as she wanted to meet him too. She missed her home too much. She started searching for other internships, but one fine day, she received the mail from the same MNC which rejected her a few weeks back, saying….

"We apologize for miscommunicating your Selection Status. You have been Selected. We are elated to………"

She didn't care to read the rest… She jumped, yelled and gave tight hugs to her mom and Pa. She even posted the same on her social media handles. Her dream (Phase 1) was right in front of her. It was just a few more weeks and she would join the team, but in a different city. Her BF got in some other metro though. But, she was too occupied with her selection status to give a damn about any other stuff around. Dreams make us selfish at times, not sure if it's for the greater good though. She replied to them and also looped in her campus head for the same. Now, she was displayed on the result board too. Her hard work paid off again, but she had to fly back to sign docs and do the paperwork. So, She waved back at her guy and homies and left. Same flight, same kind of boarding, (obviously, it will be the same) window seat and same teary-eyed moment hit her. Three years back, the way she looked at her city; nothing changed, but again, many changed. It's always a maze that way.

She reached the campus and received many surprise parties arranged by her guy friends and obviously, other female friends too. Her guy sent her many food items and small cute presents through courier and kept on surprising her. Maybe that was the first time, she entered another's Amazing club *(Reminder: HAC).* She finished all her projects and phase tests and all other *stupid* formalities needed. It was summer vacation, but not really for Her. Instead of vacation, it's all about internship in another city and staying away from mom and Pa and of course, Her BF. Since the day they started dating, there was never a phase where they stayed together more than a month. But, they pulled it off really well. Credits to smart-ass girl and guy too!

Chapter- 3

She reached the new city, posted all the online formalities. It was a huge corporate building or tower or office or….who cared… It was Huge, that's it! She couldn't stop staring at the skyscrapers around. It seemed like flying abroad for Her. She was just twenty-year-old; nothing wrong with overwhelming. She ran around and explored the CCD and other coffee places. Many breweries were around offices to chill workplaces. She felt it too much for the day. She distracted Herself and reached her floor. Well, TBH, it took more than fifteen minutes just to find the exact building. All of them looked similar to Her. She needed a lot of help which included many calls to the HR team, five colleagues, and others too. Then she realized she might be born over matured, but not smart enough to know this XYZ building. She finished the paperwork, orientation program, and introduction to her team. Her first day went so hectic that she wanted to fall on her king-size mattress so badly. But, she had no luck. As soon as she reached, phone rang. First, it was mom and then Pa…(no clue why parents have no coordination in this aspect, they always call separately!! Why??). Third, it was Her guy. She was forced to respond to their calls. Then she rested and rested. Initially, Corporate life gave her a real high, but later a hit and a reality check; not easy at all. But, She got used to it and gave in to Her weekends just to rest and laze around in her room. At times, she had to report on Sundays too. Yuck! Jeez! Hats off to her nods and patience! Two months pass by similarly with lots of work with very less weeks off, even lesser leaves, but lots of learning. She could not meet her homies as She reached her campus directly. She missed them so bad for the past two months; horse riding, car rides, her Pa and his biz meets. All were compromised for a while. It was her final year. No clue how three years passed by so easily for Her. Events… friends… vacations… relationships… part-time work… everything passed through her mind during her flight journey. She might be very smart, over-matured or talented… but not a rock. She cried so bad sitting in the restroom. She hated it more as the washrooms on the flight weren't comfy enough to rest her bum. It was so congested that she had to wipe her tears and rush into her aisle seat immediately. Once she reached her hostel, she knew all of that were going to be one-last-time or one-last-year kind of stuff. She emoted it that way. But placements were speeding too fast; just a few more weeks. She ain't even sure if her internship people would call her back (PPO). Corporate life is very wavering ...one never knows. Supply... demand... budget... NAV... all of them becoming deciding factors in a jiffy rather than the work she did. She started preparing alongside Her friends. This time, she was accompanied by her friends to the library. Placements are the only reason which attracts reputed colleges. FACTS. Hence, everyone worked their asses off in the final year, come what may. After all, they needed a job before leaving the campus.

One fine day....

Him: Sup

Her: Busy

Him: Has been many months. Want to meet you.

Her: Study. Both of us have placement stuff coming soon.

Him: I know. I am aware of the same. I have been doing the same. BYE.

Her: I am sorry. I am busy. I will call you for sure, but let things get sorted first.

Him: Hmm. Byeee.

Tough nut! She was indeed that. None could deny Her. None could accept her hundred per cent too. But, none could avoid her too. She was a weird, tough blend of all of these. Hence, he survived the relationship. Placement week started and they went on for eight days; The first day, first shot; nothing worked for her. Second... third... fourth... Thirty per cent of the campus got placed. She wasn't. The next day, her BF was placed too; no luck for Her though. She lost hope day by day. She had no clue about the patterns. She soon realized, most of the time it's Luck, that matters in placements. She immediately sent an email to her internship company for feedback. That was entirely against her campus policies. She dared to do it, as She had no other option. But, she created her own fate like every time. She received the reply after two days ...

"We are elated to announce PPO to ..."

That mail was sent directly to the campus, and not to her. So, they had no clue that She sent an email to HR earlier. Neither has the HR team mentioned the same to the campus. It was unknown to anyone except Her. Daring at times works a lot. Her life had been used to *be daring*. So, for Her, dare worked the most. In fact, she got placed with one of the highest packages on the campus. As soon as the campus got to know the news, her bestie, mom, Pa, Her guy and everyone was informed by one or the other. Both of them were placed, and he couldn't stop, but flew back to Her. He met her, greeted her and surprised her. This time, she surprised him...

Him: Where are you taking me?

Her: Just come.

Him: Tell me.

Her: Look at your mail.

Him: I hardly open them, at least after I got placed I don't.

Her: LOL. Just do it.

Him: A biz plan! Who helped you with this?

Her: Did you like it?

Him: IDK. I mean I have no words, baby. I mean how do you manage all of this? I mean how do you get the time? I mean... IDK. This is all crazy.

She was really smart… smarter… smartest. Self-managed kid! She had no response to his queries though. She spent time on the weekends during her internship… after getting PPO, after all the tensions, she definitely could build a plan that way. It wasn't a big deal for Her for sure. The plan she came up with had lots of research done on their future biz. This might take four-five years. But She was so sure about the typical question, *"Where do you see yourself in the next five years?"* Almost every student faces it during their interview. That was one of the most hated questions by them though. Like one never knew what's going to happen this week… next week… month… year… and even the next moment, then how would one be able to detect one's future for five years? She was definitely weird or different. She was sure about her next five years. She was sure about Her next month… moment and year. At least, nothing was wrong with having a view of ourselves for the next five years. That's her POV. If it didn't work, there would always be a backup plan according to Her. So, she spent the time planning Her future no theirs to be precise, but she wouldn't mind including him. Their ROI, biz ventures, budget, partnerships, IPO, and all business terms were included in the plan. But, he had no clue about fifty percent of the terms used by Her. She seemed like some MBA grad rather than a B-tech graduate, to him. For sure she was born over-matured or maybe with skills none could have at her age. At times, she *Is* and *Was* better than her seniors too. But it was a shocker for him.........

Him: Are you normal?

Her: Oh please! Jeez! Finally, even you ended up asking me this.

Him: Baby. I was kidding. I wanted to pull your leg. Chill.

Her: You can, but not in this aspect.

Him: Are you fine?

Her: I have been fine. But, not that, you know every moment, I faced like through my friends or relatives or other strangers. There were always situations that pulled me down. I was born over matured, at least, that's what everyone called me. They were amazed by the stuff, I used to do. But, I was always stuck in a maze if that was a pro or a con on my end, because my parents used to be over protective. They were embarrassed, scared, even felt bad about it. I ain't complaining about all of this, because I care about these the least. And in fact, that's the only reason I chose to date you. You treated me very normal or ended up appreciating me. You never were that person who was shocked, surprised and ended up ignoring me. Thanks, baby! You deserve to know my plan.

Him: Hmm... Our?

Her: Hahahahhahah. Love you.

She gave him a peck and left from there. The next evening, they met and went to their regular spot; beach and biryani hotel. They ate like their last moment on Earth. It was out of happiness, excitement, and contentment. They realized it had been almost one and half years of their togetherness and there they were planning their next five years. That made Her emotional, and she cried after having two beers. She couldn't stop, but puke it, confessed it and all the stuff that she dumped inside her. She even mentioned how she handled racism at times. It was like *Confession Day* for Her and *Taking Confessions Day* for him. He had no clue how to react. He was even angry that she hid all of these. He never hid stuff and always shared every bit of his emotions with her.

Him: Why would you hide all of this??

Her: As if I wanted to!

Him: Then?

Her: I was waiting for the right moment. Not like I have cheated on you!

Him: LOL. Relax. Now on...every feeling should be shared with me. My humble request, baby.

Her: You too.

Him: I have always done that. You know that!

Her: Hmmm. Let's leave. It's time for your flight's take-off.

Him: This sucks. I think after a few months when we start working I will make sure we live in the same house.

Her: How?

Him: I will request my HR for a transfer.

Her: Sulk Pot.

Him: Stop it.

Her: Hahhhhhahah.

They left. He flew back after tight hugs. This time, it was more emotional for him post all the facts, she spoke about. Biz plan... future... racism... he felt like a new dictionary hit him.. But, he regretted not knowing or guessing that She went through all of that, earlier. Tough shit!

As soon as she reached Her room, she observed a pamphlet right in front of her cot. It displayed horse riding classes. She called the number on the pamphlet and bargained for prices. She ended up getting a decent offer. She imagined herself on a horse. It was like riding a horse after almost a year. She missed it way too much. And, also no one knew that she could do the same as none of her social media handles had it. Only her mom, Pa and her BF knew that skill of hers. She woke up at 4 am daily and left for the classes. Her friends had no clue but it's tough to hide it for a longer time. After a few weeks, she got caught. Her bestie couldn't just stop but ran to her and asked her the reason. She had to tell the entire story of her habits and Her liking for horse riding, like how a scriptwriter details it to an actor. It's obvious that her bestie was left in awe. She was speechless. She took a minute to say words… something… anything…

Bestie: Is there a moment that you never hid or didn't end up making me feel like "OMG"?

Her: Actually…

Bestie: Shut up and get lost. There is no sense in befriending a girl like you.

Her: I am sorry. I was scared.

Bestie: Of me? Sorry... yourself? LOL.

Her: I thought all of you might end up judging me. Most of the people I know always saw me as this *"extra matured or over matured female"*. I don't want to judge or be judged either.

Bestie: But you got to trust me, at least, ME !!!! It's me !!!! Me !!!!

Her: It's you !!! LOL. I know.

Bestie: Get lost.

She had to let go of Her bestie for a while. She gave that space to her. In fact, half of the campus got to know. They were all amazed and thrilled. Many even ended up joining the classes. But still, she had no clue about the mystery behind that pamphlet in her room. None knew who left it there. The coaching centre felt Her as their new brand ambassador as all her college mates joined through her. None even knew that the classes existed before she joined. First, it spread as a rumor... then news... facts... joining classes. The entire chain benefited only the company and no one else. Well, she was clicked and papped by the team, and her face was all over their websites and social media handles. She was that *famous kid* now. Her city knew her even more. Her mom was, as usual, scared though...

Mom: What is all that news?

Her: Yeah, thanks!

Mom: I ain't praising or appreciating you!!

Her: I want to be an optimistic soul. Hahahaha!

Mom: I hate your sarcastic tone, now. You better stop responding this way.

Her: What's wrong with these marketing schemes? I am their new brand ambassador. They are paying me. I ain't modeling or something for you to be worried.

Mom: I wish you did that. At least, you would wear lots of makeup and be even more famous. But, this coaching centre seems like a cheap one. Cheapskates!

Her: Stop it.

She hung up the call. She just loathed the entire conversation. Sometimes, her mom was too good to even guess, but at times, she was the weirdest one. That's how she felt and left the class. She loved going there and doing marketing for the company. Nothing else mattered; obviously, they paid well. Her BF even loved her posters on their online handles. He even promoted his girl on his social media platforms. Well, he got famous too. One day, she received a call from her HR…

Her: Hello ma'am. How are you?

HR: I am good. How about you?

Her: Likewise. Thanks. Yes, tell me.

HR: I have seen your face on a brand poster for their coaching classes. I need to discuss something on that.

Her: Sure. *(She was scared, as fuck)*

HR: Actually, I was looking for horse riding coaching for my son. He loves it, but we can't afford the prices. Can you have a word and get better pricing if possible?

She: Sure. I will revert soon. *(Laughing inside so badly)*

Post the call, she called her BF and explained the same. They laughed out so loud that they had to stop, else they might faint. It was that hilarious. She soon realized that Her bestie was still pissed at her even after many weeks. She tried talking to her, but nothing worked. Giving little space makes sense, but too much space for too many days won't make sense. She didn't want her college days to end in a way where she would end up in other people's bad books; especially, in Her besties' book. Farewell was just a few weeks ahead. They were all busy with their project work while their juniors got busy in arranging, planning and organizing *farewell*. She didn't want college life to end as Her bestie would be leaving the country soon. Her bestie came on NRA quota which meant she would be leaving anytime soon. She decided to surprise her. She spoke with the coaching classes and asked for a dual-face promotion so that she could do it with her bestie, and they agreed to it. She took the contract and ran to her bestie to show the same. Her bestie liked it so much that it got tough to avoid Her. She couldn't be tough on Her anymore.

Her: I am sorry. And, no more talking. We have a shoot tomorrow.

Bestie: Me too. I am really sorry. I was a bit harsh for the past few months. But you are over-smart this way. You got me this offer and cooled me down.

Her: LOL. Let's go now.

They rushed to the shooting spot and gave amazing pictures to the marketing team. Now, they were together on the websites. She felt satiated as things got sorted that way. Her mom called her again….

Mom: So, next time, is it with a guy? Your BF?

Her: Can you stop? Why can't you behave normally?

Mom: Relax. I was kidding. I loved you both on the covers.

Her: You better be. Bye

She even hated lifting the call if it was her mom. *Well, it's just a few more months, and I will be out of the campus; in a new city and new life with my BF.* She had the final project and assignment submissions. She soon realized that now it's her shoots, submissions, pampering her bestie, farewell, HR son's discounted stuff and everything piled up in her head, and Her day journal too. She hated pending stuff and hence, decided to work on them. Though few were done, the rest were terrifying. Her submissions were like never before. Every B-Tech student could feel this; the last semester felt like hundreds of arrears even to the toppers like Her. Too many deadlines just push one so bad that he / she might throw up. The adrenaline rush hit you harder in the last few weeks.

Finally, the farewell party was on! And, she looked like a cynosure for every other junior and batchmate. Even her guy guessed that and ended up attending Her college farewell. Though it wasn't legal she smuggled him into the campus. She wore simple bodycon black attire and made others feel *"Nerds do look hot"*. She wasn't just a nerd! Those who knew her *knew her*. Her guy couldn't stop pulling her closer and they danced expecting it to be a Prom which wasn't in reality! They boozed and chilled; she dragged him to Her hostel which was a challenging task though; it was a co-ed hostel, but dragging drunk people ain't a small task at all! He just stared at all the organized corners, their pics stamped on her desk, many more attractive things; he felt half sober, looking at Her OCD phases! But, she distracted him and pulled him to Her, and they got some privacy for a night! The next morning, she had a flight, but this time, they both were flying back together. It was just a few weeks before she would have to stay at Her home. So, as soon as she reached her home, she spent a lot of time with her Pa and Her mom.

Mom: So, B-Tech done!

Her: Yes, finally, no more coconut oil.

Mom: LOL. Well, I can still cook using the same, though.

Her: I will abandon you. Hahaha.

Mom: Ahh??

Her: No more jokes with coconut oil.

Mom: So tell me, what next?

Her: I got a PPO, and I will be moving to a new city very soon. Hope you don't have any memory issues, Mrs. Mom.

Mom: Mrs. Mom?! What's wrong with your English?

Her: Relax.

Mom: Well, I and Pa were planning to move with you.

She froze as she took two-three minutes to decipher it. She had no response, but she had to respond or else her ability to not respond might make *them* respond more. Her mom might feel dubious and exhibit all her spy skills. So, she tried to act normally.

Her: Nice. But, I don't want anyone around. Got to focus on my career.

Mom: LOL.

Her: As in?

Mom: We want to protect you, kid!

Her: Thanks for the concern. I said that I want to do things on my own.

Mom: Your dad will handle it. As usual, I always fail at this.

Her: Yes you do. Perfect. I know how to convince my Pa.

Mom: Lol. He was the one who suggested this. Just letting you know.

She froze again. She had no response againnnnnnnn. In fact, she was scared if Her Pa got to know about her dating life or any sort of that. She wasn't sure. Firstly, she has to cross-check with her Pa. *Indirectly*.

Her: Sup

Pa: Hello kid. How come you wake up so soon even on a holiday?

Her: I wish I were that girl.

Pa: Just kidding. Everyone knows you. What happened?

Her: Heard the update from Mom.

Pa: What kind of update, kid?

Her: You both moving in and stuff?

Pa: Oh yeah. Thanks. That was my plan.

Her: Thanks for what? I ain't okay with it, firstly. I want to be myself in a new city. Secondly...

Pa: Good. We will just protect you. I can manage all the biz from there too. I know you are worried about me. Don't? Relax!

Her: Stop talking about protecting me and all. I ain't a kid now.

Pa: I don't want to argue on this. Just leave.

"Just leave" from Her Pa was like a harbinger to shut up. She had to leave and saw Her mom smirking. That was the first time, She lost it to her mom. Now, *She* had to start some spy-level planning and stuff. She had to make sure they won't accompany Her. She was not sure how, but that's Her mission and she had just two weeks' time. She even asked her BF to help her on that, otherwise their plan to stay together would be aborted. They had been waiting for this, for a while. TBH, almost two years! She called her bestie and asked for help. Though she was smart enough

to do that on her own, she didn't want to take any risk and asked them for help. In fact, Her BF was also responsible to handle the situation, not just hers. She kept thinking of a really tough one, as her mom was a good spy. Her mom had a good experience in that too; in her childhood, she spied on Her a lot. She could never get rid of those moments. It was like a trio mission with Herself, Her BF, and her bestie on board. They had a group on social media handles and surfed for movies, books, and stories to blend a few and execute the mission. They were all sure about Her mom's skills which could never be underestimated. Parallelly, Her mom was caught up with lots of shopping and packing. Day by day, Her heart thumped even faster.

One fine day, she woke up at 3 AM and died of thirst. She rushed to the fridge and had gallons of water. Soon, she realized her dream. Thanks to that though! It was about her lying about the location. Though the *real* people couldn't help her with a plan, Her dream could. She waited for her parents to wake up, which took three hours.

Her: Pa. Bad news.

Pa: What happened, kid? Waking up itself sucks and don't dump more stuff that sucks.

Her: My location got shifted, I suppose.

Pa: But?

She mentioned a city name which for sure her Pa or mom wouldn't want to live in.

Pa: OMG! That's too far. Pretty sure, I won't be able to pull off my biz from there. How will you stay there?

Her: Exactly. You guys stay back. It's fine. I have no other options.

Pa: No worries. I will job hunt for you.

She thought *Fuck. I think this is gonna backfire.*

Her: Not needed. I love this company, and I am moving there. We will job hunt after a few months.

Pa: Fine. But sorry, that we won't be able to make it to it.

She was shocked that Her Pa fell for her stuff. Guilty though. *Whatever, I am a free bird now*. But, her mom wouldn't fall for this shit though. So, She was all prepared to convince her mom, which definitely needed extra effort. Once her mom woke up and got to know the shifting update which was *that shifting won't be possible*, she became that typical mom who felt everything was dubious. She asked for proofs like location shift approval from HR, new city details and whatnot! Well, She being a smart-ass could expect it and had all docs handy (well, she edited them using online tools). Her mom couldn't doubt that aspect though. She might be clever, but not a techie. In the end, it was a happy ending. All fell for Her stuff and she started packing while Her mom unpacked. It was super fun for Her to watch her mom do this. She did enact that She felt bad that their parents had to drop it off. Didn't overact, just acted or else the Spy agent would be on board for another mission aka Her mom. It was just a few more days for them to move in. They had all the stay, travel, and shopping done.

Once they landed to new city, new phase... New! New! New!... it was the only word revolving in her head. She wasn't sure if it was a good or bad sign. The new flat, new job and new people around; she loved every bit of it. He was more than excited. They had a few more days left to join their work, but chose to travel and shift before the same so that they get some time to spend together. They went around for groceries. She gave all guidelines to him on how to maintain the house as she had major OCD levels. Not that, he wasn't aware, but she loved to torture him by reminding him about Her OCD. She decorated her room so well that he hated his room. Though it was a live-in they planned to have their own rooms. She always maintained that dignity and independence; come what may. They had good neighbours around who were party animals. Well, he was happy with them but not sure about her. She loved partying though but not like an animal.

Day one of their jobs was there and they both woke up to laziness. None felt like leaving but had to, for money. He cooked a good brekkie for her post which they left in their own modes of transport. She had fun meeting colleagues; few college mates who ended up in the same role and company and the HR-TA team. Her manager was a tough nut though. Her corporate life started like a cliche one with BF waiting at home; manager dumping work; neighbours partying every night; going back to cooking for herself. A few weeks went by so happily, weekends too; shopping….making out… cooking… movies… dinner nights… dates. It was a blend of all sorts of live-in. But, there was always the tail that followed the good moments. In fact, She was also worried about the same. But, not sure when that would hit. Slowly, she observed changes in their bond like fights were observed frequently. Both of their schedules were real hectic due to which they ended up arguing even for the minute things. She didn't like it nor did he. But again, they hardly had time to even discuss what they were going through. They knew it but ended up ignoring it. She loathed it and decided to call it off one fine day…..

Her: I have to discuss something.

Him: Sure. Shoot!

Her: It has been troubling me for a few weeks, but today I have to puke it out.

Him: I said shoot!

Her: I think we should stay away for a while for the greater good.

Him: As in? A break?

Her: Yes, but we can patch up later. I feel it's going too rough.

Him: Even I felt the same, but according to me, there is no break just a breakup.

Her: Kewl. If you want the same let's call it off.

Him: I never said I wanted that. I said I don't believe in breaks and patch-ups. In fact, that's why I broke up with my ex. She always wanted breaks.

Her: I think break works for me. If not, I am ready to call it off.

No more replies from his end, and he banged the door. He locked himself in and hated the fight. The next day, they called it off and parted ways. So, now, it was again a new life; home phase for Her but this time, with loads of pain. She couldn't stay stable. A smart-ass like her was tough to be beaten emotionally but not in front of a relationship. Even the toughest people face pain in Love. None can escape; no privileges for anyone when it's Love. She got her HRs approval for shifting back to Her city and stayed home. She tried to keep Herself sane; horse riding, sports, gym nothing helped. She even met a shrink for help. She soon realized she went into depression. There was nothing that could excite Her for real and simultaneously, nothing that could bring her down except Love and Live-in. She didn't expect the latter one though. She went on a digital detox on every social media platform of Hers. She didn't hate him but never wanted to meet him for sure. Her bestie called her many times for the same. She tried to patch Her up with her so-called BF. But, She didn't react. She kept silent and didn't respond at all. She blindly followed her shrink, in fact that was the first time, she followed someone and Blindly !!

She hated this life shift and mind set change. All of which were influenced by a single emotion and a single person. She wasn't herself anymore, but thanks to Her work life, she wasn't affected at all.

In fact, that was the best distraction for Her. Though her personal life was racked with pain, it was Her professional life that helped her move on. Few months passed by similarly; just her job, her parents, her beanbags, and her home. She completely got isolated from the world. Well, that wasn't something her shrink suggested. It was a self-choice that way. She even tried to move on but could not connect with anyone around. When nothing worked, books did. She brought back her nerd mode. But, this time, it wasn't for any grades or any ranks or any kind of admissions or appreciation; it wasn't for anything except for Her peace. She missed her humor, her smartness, her patience; she became an entirely different person. She spent half of her savings on books. Like maximum genres were covered in less than three months. Hundreds of books; many book marathons; many book events; book fairs. She covered all that she could. Though all of that didn't let her move on, it lessened Her suffering. It did exactly what she wanted for Herself. She could feel her revival state. She soon decided to take a week off for a solo trip. One of the books inspired Her to be wanderlust for a while. She got all the approvals from Her HR and manager, but a mission was needed to convince Her mom. Well, somehow she managed it. This time, it was Goa but no company. *It was just She, Her, and Herself.*

She took a flight and landed. Collected her baggage and directly hit the beach even before boarding the hotel. She could see only a few tourists around and the blue waves dominated and grabbed her attention though. Clean water, waves, sounds. She immediately ran to her bag and grabbed a notepad. She started writing down some random lines. Like she had no clue what she was into, but all she could see was her pen and fingers going non-stop for 40 minutes. They sped up parallelly with her thoughts and feelings. Post the beach visit, she went to a bar and chilled for a while having a pint; all for Herself. She could realize her buzz levels and craved a nap and finally ended up in the hotel. She rested and woke up the next morning. She had a really bad hangover and wanted to rest more but had to check her phone which had an infinite number of missed calls; all from her obvious well-wisher, MOM! She just texted her back and ignored the calls. Then she opened her notepad which had like thousands of words and sentences. She read them and yelled so loud that the hospitality team banged on Her door. She had to convince them later saying *nothing happened.* Well, she was good at such a smart way of lying. But why did she yell, though?

Right away She called her bestie (which was after many months)......

Her: Hey. I need to tell you something.

Bestie: Wow! Finally!

Her: I know you loathe me to death. You can hate me later. But you need to listen to this.

Bestie: You ghosted me and...

Her: Wait... I said later. You have my entire time to hate me and scold me.

Bestie. Thanks! Shoot!

Her: I want to be an author.

Bestie: What? An author for textbooks and educational stuff? LOL.

Her: Very funny. Shut up. I can Write! Do you get that?

Bestie: Then write, my dear. Who can stop you?

Her: I wish you were better than this. Get lost. Bye

She hated Herself for even sharing the info with her bestie. She later enjoyed her solo travel by meeting new friends, wanderlust, photo dumping through Instax, and a lot more! Writing down added a lot of flavor to Her trip. It was something out of nowhere. Like some random toaster notification on a phone display. Once her trip was done, she reached her place. And discussed the same with Her Pa. She even showed the blurb of her book and a few phrases that she included in her writings. He couldn't agree more about Her becoming an author. She never had a blog never read thousands of books; .never knew more than forty authors and never had the thought of writing. But, here she was soon planning to launch her book with the help of Her company too. Her team, manager, HR, and everyone loved the blurb. So, they didn't mind collaborating with her to publish it. All of that just happened in a few weeks. She worked on the same every day for at least three hours. She even ended up getting a few leeway from her team so that she could spend time on her writing. She reached out to many authors and other social media influencers and shared the blurb. Though few didn't like it, most of them loved it and encouraged Her. That way, She planned to get the marketing help on board. Few publishers mailed her post the blurb shared with them. They were more than surprised to see a twenty-four-year-old writing such amazing and mature stuff. It was the perks of over-matured-ly born kids.

She finally finished her plot, book, approvals, agreements, and proofreading. In fact, the launch date was close. One fine day, she woke up and fainted. When she woke up she saw herself in a hospital bed. Her mom and Pa were eagerly looking at Her. But, it was just a panic attack. Even She could feel nothing wrong with her, physically or mentally; it was just her parents exaggerating things. She immediately checked her phone which was loaded with sympathy-empathy messages from so many that she had to just seen zone them instead of replying. She felt completely normal and wanted to get ready for her launch. She wanted to be prepared mentally, until her mom denied the same. The latter became overprotective of her kid which irked Her so much. Her PMS hit her so bad that she even yelled at Her doctor. She left from there despite all the refusals and denials. Finally, She reached her home, room, space, and corner. She slept on the beanbags for hours without her conscience. She just wanted to stay alone. She had no clue what to talk about or discuss in her launch. She went to her Pa that night…

Her: Pa… I don't want to attend the launch. I am kind of nervous.

Pa: LOL. This ain't my kid at all. I hope the medication didn't twist you this way.

Her: I am serious. For Pete's sake!!

Pa: Look. Just go to your bed and once recollect all the moments you faced in your life, the most challenging ones. I would love to remind you a few though; your SPL time, your Sports Head times, your event handling times. My memory ain't that good to remind you more than this. Hahaha. But also one thing you might have felt bad when I and your mom were overprotective about your skills. Maybe, we even felt it embarrassing, just imagine how you handled such tough times. I know we weren't that good back then, but I promise you, kid, we will never be such parents. You have no clue how much we regret those days.

Her: Pa…..you need not be. Please stop saying that. In fact, you both were worried about the criticism that I would have to face and hence you chose to be overprotective. I know it might not have been the perfect solution. But no use in discussing what has been done. Nothing can be undone or redone. So, let's discuss something useful.

Pa: Wow! I feel like my mom or dad talking. I mean you changed a lot, my dear. Proud of you. Good Night!

She went back to her room and did what her Pa suggested. She jotted down all Her tough moments, challenging roles, leadership stuff, She had done in her past. She was amazed at the way;

it worked. She soon gained a lot of hope and confidence. That night, She slept peacefully. She slept like there was no next day, morning, Book launch and speech. The next morning She woke up to all good vibes. She felt like she had so many spiritual sessions from Her Pa. She rushed to Her restroom and went to her mom for a brekkie. All that she did the first time she went to school, she did the same way. She could even juxtapose them and smiled to herself. She gave a huge hug to her mom and Pa. Her mom was teary-eyed though. She didn't have time to soothe Her mom and hence she left. She asked her Pa to soothe Her mom, instead. Few things just don't change. And it shan't too.

She could see, at least sixty-seventy strangers around. She had no clue about them. Her HR, manager, a few other colleagues, publishers and many other known faces were also present. *I called them for formality and they took it so seriously that they ended up here. How lame!* She then reached the stage and was shivering. But realized what her Pa said. Out of nowhere, she could see Her mom and Pa right in the front row. She understood that might have been their way of surprising Her. She went to the podium, held the mic, greeted everyone present there, and went on....

I have never thought I would be here this way.

Like an author

Like having an official book launch

Like having to see many people around me

Like reviving from my broken past

Like receiving lots of applause even before the launch

Like many authors who loved my blurb

Like many more to come though

Thanks for everything.

She felt like a star post the dispersal. She got papped and posed with many of them at the launch. Once She reached home she slept and never wanted to wake up. Little did she know that her adrenaline rush was gonna hit her soon. After a few weeks, when she was at the office, Her phone kept ringing and she had to take it. It was from the publishing house and they wanted to discuss the royalty and sales of the books. They even wanted to conduct a successful event as the book's reach went global. It was beyond what she expected it to be, though.

She reached the event with her parents and everyone stared at Her, Her book, Her thoughts and Her emotions. She was so grateful that she ended up showing it through her tears. She had no words as everything was gifted. At least, that's how she felt. Though her hard work paid her huge, a bit of luck was added up too. Later she delivered a speech, but it was very crisp and short. Then a few of the students over there approached Her for pics, autographs, and whatnot!! She gave them accordingly. Then she saw a guy who called her out and asked for an autograph. To Her surprise it was HIM!!! She just stared at him and felt numb. Like she had nothing to say but throw Him a soft smile gave the autograph, shook hands side hug and left from there. She felt complete, that day.

But what was in Her book so good that everyone loved it including Her ex-BF?

Well, she was born over-matured, and she used it to Her best.

That night's sleep was the most accountable one she ever had.

It was just She, *Her and Herself.*

Acknowledgements

I would love to thank every living being who has been part of my journey to date which includes my parents for my birth, my friends for irking me, my enemies for enlightening me, my critics for pushing me for better, my pets, my editors, and my publishing house.

OrangeBooks was not just helpful but family since day one of my collaboration with them. Young talent can be made public and given exposure, only through platforms like these.

Huge thanks to my Dad for listening to my drafts, and plots and for encouraging me, come what may.

Thanks to all those who read books in front of me and made me go like how can one read such fat books?

Thanks to all who felt my diction was typical through which I made sure to keep my book as simple as possible.

My only goal is and has been to make sure my reader base /audience read my book with ease and comfort with little struggle.

Thanks to Covid *in a weird manner* which made me a book lover, book writer and much more!

Happy Reading!!!

www.ingramcontent.com/pod-product-compliance
Lightning Source LLC
LaVergne TN
LVHW061343080526
838199LV00093B/6922